WINNING
VOLLEYBALL
FOR GIRLS

Second Edition

DEBORAH W. CRISFIELD

MARK GOLA

Foreword by
STACY SYKORA
U.S. Women's Olympic Volleyball Team

A MOUNTAIN LION BOOK

Checkmark Books®
An imprint of Facts On File, Inc.

WINNING VOLLEYBALL FOR GIRLS, Second Edition

Checkmark Books
An imprint of Facts On File, Inc.
132 West 31st Street
New York, NY 10001

Library of Congress Cataloging-in-Publication Data

Crisfield, Deborah.
    Winning volleyball for girls / Deborah W. Crisfield ; foreword by Stacy
    Sykora.—2nd ed.
        p. cm.
    "A Mountain Lion book."
    Includes bibliographical references and index.
    ISBN 0-8160-4620-4 (hard : alk. paper)—ISBN 0-8160-4621-2 (pbk : alk. paper)
    1. Volleyball for girls. I. Title.
    GV1015.4.W66 C75 2002
    796.325—dc21   2001033473

Text design by Erika K. Arroyo
Cover design by Nora Wertz

Printed in the United States of America

VB FOF 10 9 8 7 6 5 4

This book is printed on acid-free paper.

CONTENTS

ACKNOWLEDGMENTS

The authors would like to extend a special thanks to the following people, without whom this book would not have been possible: Diane Herbst; the Paramus Catholic girls volleyball team and head coach Ed Saggio; John Monteleone, photographer; Gavin D. Markovitz, Public Relations Director for USA Volleyball and Stacy Sykora for her foreword.

FOREWORD

I come from a small town outside of Fort Worth, Texas, called Burleson. I grew up playing volleyball there, and as early as second grade, I dreamed of competing in the Olympic Games.

I spent my entire childhood in Burleson, and I thought I might never leave, until I was offered an athletic scholarship to play volleyball at Texas A&M University. After playing four years of volleyball at the collegiate level, I trained with the United States national team in Colorado Springs for a year and a half. I played in the World University Games before competing on the U.S. national team. Finally, I was part of the fourth place–finishing USA Olympic team in Sydney, Australia.

Sounds like a simple, smooth ride, doesn't it? A young girl dreams of playing in the Olympics, and she suits up in a team USA uniform in Sydney, Australia, years later. I wish things were that easy, but, believe me, the higher you set your mountain tops, the steeper the climb.

I can recall how frustrating my first practice was at Texas A&M. I was extremely intimidated by my new teammates and their skills. In high school, everything came easy to me. I was always the "go-to" girl who never needed to learn proper fundamentals or the meaning of the game of volleyball. I went back to my room that day overwhelmed by fear and anxiety. I sat out in the hall and cried for hours, realizing how much I needed to learn. I had suddenly discovered that volleyball was not just about hitting the ball straight down; it's about technique, mental preparation, and teamwork.

I accepted the challenge to improve, and I went on to have a great collegiate career, thanks largely to Texas A&M head coach Laurie Corbelli and assistant coach John Corbelli. After college, I was given the opportunity to train with the U.S. national team during a six-month tryout. Hearing the news of that opportunity was the happiest day of my life. In retrospect, it's funny how life seems to repeat itself—my first day of practice with the national team was identical to the one I'd experienced four years before in college. The international game is a huge step up from the college level. I was the second libero (international term for defensive position) on the team behind a two-year veteran. This was difficult for me because I'd never been behind someone at my position. I was sent to the World University Games (WUG) to be the libero for that team while Laura Davis, the other libero, maintained the starting spot for the U.S. national team at the time.

I was devastated. After a week of playing with the WUG team, however, I was called back to the United States because Laura had hurt her ankle and they needed a replacement. A window of opportunity opened up for me, and I never looked back.

After a great experience with the national team, I earned a ticket to Sydney by being named to the United States Women's Olympic Volleyball team. I cried all day because *this* was now the happiest day of my life. We placed fourth in Sydney, losing the bronze medal match to Brazil. The fourth-place finish was a memorable achievement since we entered the tournament as the tenth seed. It was a once-in-a-lifetime experience that I will cherish for the rest of my life.

I am a small town girl who has traveled the world. I had a dream that started as a child, and once it was in sight, I never lost sight of it. It would have been easy to give up or to settle for what I had already accomplished, but I refused to allow myself to stop setting new goals.

I've made many choices in my life, most of them good and some very difficult. I paid a lot of dues, but in the end, I have no regrets and I make no excuses. Everyone who has a dream needs to ask themselves one question, "Why not me?" Why not the girl from Burleson, Texas? I put on my shoes, breath the same air, and play the same sport as the other girls. I learned that no one cares who you were until you are someone—you have to care about you.

Volleyball has made me laugh, cry, bleed, and ache. It's kept me in a gym instead of being out with my friends; it's kept me away from my family; and it's taken me to countries where the food can walk off your plate. In the end, I have memories I will keep for a lifetime and would not change for the world. What began as a fun sport for me to play as a child grew into a career, a job, and a love.

Keep Dreamin'
No Regrets
No Excuses

—Stacy Sykora
United States Women's
Olympic Volleyball Team

INTRODUCTION

Among high school girls, volleyball is the second most popular sport, right behind basketball. The interest in the sport has sky-rocketed, yet there is no solid resource on the bookshelves to help coaches and players at this level improve and refine their game. *Winning Volleyball for Girls* fills that void. Written for both players and coaches, the book is a comprehensive source that covers all aspects of the game, from rules, to training, to winning that 15th point.

If you read this book and take it to heart, you'll soon be DIGGING, SPIKING, TIPPING, BLOCKING, and ROLLING like a pro. You'll know all about SIDING OUT, WIPING OFF, and scoring kills. And you'll be an accomplished, knowledgeable volleyball player or coach.

This book is not for picnic volleyball players. In picnic volleyball, players just slap the ball back and forth over the net. In competitive high school volleyball, however, there's always a carefully planned attack and defense. Teams try to have a PASS, SET, and hit every time they are on offense, and then they go into a blocking, digging defense. All of these strategies are addressed in later chapters.

This book begins with volleyball's history, rules, court dimensions, and equipment before it discusses training and then specific skills: serving, passing, setting, spiking, and blocking. The skills appear in the order they are used in the game, and this is a great way for coaches to teach their players. For instance, if players first learn the SERVE and then move to the SERVE RECEIVE, they can do serving and passing drills. The next skill is setting, which allows players to serve, pass, and set. Each time the players add a skill, they get closer to play-ing the whole game. It's a natural progression.

Following the chapters on skills is one on offense and strategy. A point to keep in mind while you're reading this book is that the offense isn't automatically the serving team. In fact, more often than not, the serving team is on defense. While only the serving team can score a point, if the receiving team is mounting an attack, it is con-

sidered the offense. The reverse also holds true—if the serving team is trying to stop that attack, it is considered defense. And then it could switch.

Instruction on defense takes up three chapters. Chapter 9 discusses individual defense, covering the skills needed to stop the opposing team's attack. Chapter 10 covers team defense, laying out the general defensive strategy. Chapter 11 is on transition, which, as you can probably figure out from its name, is the actual process of moving from defense to offense, or vice versa.

Once you're comfortable with the different skills and strategies, you're ready to put it all together in a competitive team. Chapter 12 discusses the various ways to choose players, capitalize on the strengths of individual players, and minimize their weaknesses. This chapter describes the most effective combinations.

Chapter 13 describes various volleyball offshoots and the different games that can be created using volleyball's equipment and rules. These can be a great aid to coaching and make practicing fun, rather than routine.

After that, it's up to you. Read the book, learn the skills, and practice, practice, practice.

Note: Cross-references to the Glossary appear throughout the text in small capital letters. A term is cross-referenced only the first time it is mentioned within a chapter. Occasionally the cross-reference does not exactly match the Glossary entry's headword (this is especially true in noun and verb usages of a term), but this small discrepancy has been allowed to avoid redundancy.

1

A LOOK AT
THE GAME

FROM MINTONETTE TO VOLLEYBALL

The American people are famous around the world for being sports lovers, embracing every new fad and following their favorite teams almost obsessively. While this has been the case ever since Native Americans roamed the country playing lacrosse, sports fanaticism really took off in the late 1800s.

During this time, people in the United States were discovering the joys of team competition. Baseball had become a national craze, and football was rapidly matching it. The games were played by enthusiasts from the beginning of spring, all through the summer, to the end of fall. Then players faced a dilemma. Winter sports, such as gymnastics, wrestling, and boxing, were sadly lacking in the two areas that had made football and baseball so popular: competition and teamwork.

Athletes around the country began to try to adapt warm-weather sports into cold-weather sports. Field hockey turned into ice hockey and baseball turned into mushball, a precursor to softball. Still, people kept comparing these sports with their outdoor counterparts. Something totally new needed to be developed.

In 1891 a young YMCA instructor named James Naismith decided to invent his own game—basketball. It turned out to be exactly what the country needed. The players at the YMCA were thrilled to have found a new game that promised some of the excitement of their outdoor sports, and the instructors were thrilled because finally they had something to entertain their bored students.

One of these young instructors was a man named William G. Morgan. He played Naismith's game of basketball and loved it. When he went to work at the YMCA in Holyoke, Massachusetts, he introduced basketball to people who had never heard of the game. But Morgan encountered a problem.

Many of the people who belonged to the Holyoke YMCA were older businessmen. They liked the competition and teamwork that basketball provided, but the sport was too rough and too exhausting for them. Morgan figured that if Naismith could invent a game, so could he. Determined to invent a winter sport that would suit the older player, Morgan created what would ultimately become volleyball.

Morgan strung a tennis net between two poles, up higher than a normal net would be. He got a light rubber ball and created a game that he called mintonette. The court was small—so it wouldn't be too exhausting for the older men—and the two teams were separated by the net, so play wouldn't get too rough.

The main rule of mintonette was that the ball must never touch the ground. If it did, the other team scored a point. Players also were not allowed to catch the ball; they had to bat it over the net.

Many of the rules that are in place today came later. For instance, in mintonette players didn't rotate around the court. And under Morgan's rules, a team's players could take as many hits as they wanted before they finally sent the ball over the net, unlike today's limit of three hits per team. The net was lower too—only seven feet high—and players were allowed to reach over it to hit the ball.

As Morgan suspected, the game was a hit among his older players, and soon everybody wanted to play mintonette. One of the game's fans, Dr. Alfred Halstead, suggested that the name be switched to volleyball, because every hit was essentially a volley. The new name caught on, and so did the sport.

Because volleyball began at a YMCA, there was already a built-in network to spread the game throughout the country. Soon volleyball was being played at every YMCA. The game quickly found its way to high schools, colleges, and even factories, where it became a popular lunch-hour activity. During World War I soldiers brought it to Europe, and it spread around the world quickly after that. In 1964 it became an Olympic sport.

A major reason for volleyball's popularity is its versatility. Because it can be played in a small area, several games can fit in one gymnasium. It is tame enough for older players, but still offers plenty of excitement for the younger, more energetic competitors. And both men and women have found it can adapt nicely to their different playing styles, which were considerably more pronounced in the nineteenth century than they are now. Women wore dresses and wouldn't dream of diving on the floor, yet the game filled the need for an exciting, competitive, yet nonstrenuous game.

Today more than 14 million women play recreational volleyball in the United States, making it the number one sport for women. Now it's played year-round, both indoors and outdoors. The equipment isn't complicated or expensive, and because the ball never bounces, the court doesn't have to be perfect. It's played everywhere from playgrounds and parks, to backyard and beaches. Every level of player can be found, from casual picnic participants to expert collegiate teams.

Young players have increased their participation in competitive volleyball by 9 percent since 1994. Nearly 400,000 girls played high school volleyball in the year 2000. There are also more opportunities for women to play in college. At the Division I level, the highest level of collegiate play, there are 306 schools that offer women's volleyball in their athletic programs. It is the second most popular sport in women's collegiate athletics, behind basketball.

Beach volleyball has also become popular in the United States. Many beach volleyball tournaments are now broadcast on the ESPN television network, and former beach volleyball player and now model-actress Gabrielle Reece has become something of a spokesperson for the sport. By 1996, two-player beach volleyball was added to Olympic competition.

In February 1999, volleyball in the United States became a profession when the United States Professional Volleyball league (USPV) was created. Twelve players were chosen to form a professional touring team, dubbed the "Dream Team." They compete against international teams and top-level college programs to promote professional women's volleyball. The USPV hopes to begin play in February 2002, thus providing American female volleyball athletes with post-collegiate career opportunities.

On the international scene, the American women surpassed everyone's expectations at the 2000 Olympics in Sydney. They advanced to the bronze medal match before losing to Brazil. It was an exemplary performance by the United States team, considering that they entered the games ranked only 10th in the world—the team wasn't expected to challenge for a medal until 2004 at the earliest.

THE COURT AND EQUIPMENT

The court measures 9 meters by 18 meters, or 60 feet by 30 feet in United States measurements. It is divided in half by the CENTER LINE—where the net goes—creating a 9 meter by 9 meter square for each side. The minimum ceiling height is 26 feet, but it can go as high as the sky, which it does in outdoor volleyball. The top of the net measures 2.2 meters (or 7'4.5") from the floor for high school girls. It's

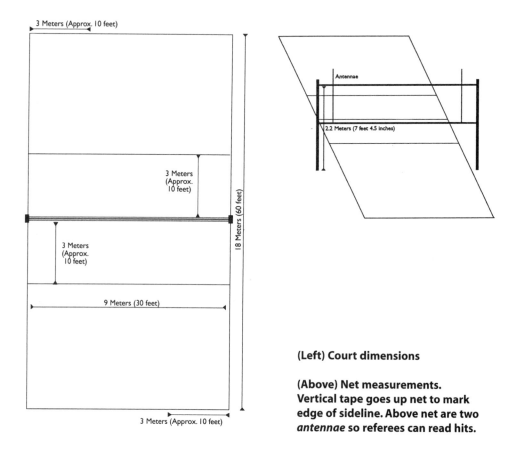

3 Meters (Approx. 10 feet)

3 Meters (Approx. 10 feet)

3 Meters (Approx. 10 feet)

9 Meters (30 feet)

18 Meters (60 feet)

3 Meters (Approx. 10 feet)

Antennae

2.2 Meters (7 feet 4.5 inches)

(Left) Court dimensions

(Above) Net measurements. Vertical tape goes up net to mark edge of sideline. Above net are two *antennae* so referees can read hits.

2.4 meters (or 8 feet) for boys. Lines are considered part of the court, so when the volleyball lands on one, it is still considered a point.

The net extends over the sidelines, so the poles are out of the court. To mark the edge of the sideline, a vertical tape goes up the net. Extending above the net are two antennae, to make it easier for the referees to read the hit.

Behind each side's end line, a 3-meter serving area is marked off. This restricts the area in which the server can move side to side. The server, however, has unlimited movement backward.

Three meters in from the center line on each side is a line that marks off the attack area. Only the players standing in that spot at the beginning of the serve are allowed to make an attack from there later in the rally.

The volleyball is a white leather ball, measuring between 25 and 27 inches around or slightly over 8 inches in diameter. It weighs about 9 ounces and should be inflated to about 5 or 6 pounds of pressure.

Aside from the ball, no additional equipment is needed, although some players like to wear elbow and knee pads.

THE RULES

The object of the game is to score 15 points (winning by 2) before the other team. Only the serving team can score a point. If the receiving team wins the rally, it does not receive a point, but it does earn the chance to serve. This is called siding out.

Play begins with a serve from the SERVING BOX behind the END LINE. The serving area includes the entire area behind the end line, from sideline to sideline. The team that wins the coin toss at the beginning decides who should serve first. The ball must cross over the net and may not hit it on the serve. A server gets only one chance to do this.

The receiving team must return the ball in three touches or less, and each touch must be clearly hit. A contact is any touch of the ball by a player, except if a player's loose hair touches the ball. If the ball touches the top knot of a ponytail or other hair near the scalp, the

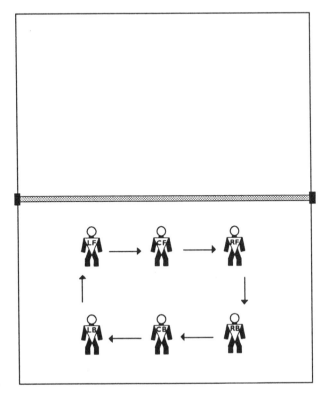

**The six positions.
Players rotate to the next
position after team sides out.**

touch is considered contact. If the ball touches the player's hair on its flight out of bounds, however, the touch would not be considered a contact. The ball may never be held, lifted, or DOUBLE HIT. Also, the same person may not hit the ball twice in a row. She may hit it twice in the same sequence, however. In other words, she may touch it the first time and the third time.

Once the ball has been returned to the serving team, the players have three touches to get it back, and so on. A BLOCK does not count as a touch.

A team wins a rally when the other team cannot return the ball over the net in three hits or less, keeping the ball within the boundaries of the court. The ball must be volleyed between or among players and across the net; it is never allowed to hit the floor.

If a player fails to make a successful volley, her team loses that particular rally. Any violation of the rest of the rules will cause a team to lose a rally. If the serving team wins the rally, it scores a point; if the nonserving team wins, it gains control of the serve but does not score a point (SIDE-OUT).

Each team has six players: the right back, the center back, the left back, the right forward, the center forward, and the left forward. Players ROTATE to the next position after the team sides out. Once the ball is served, players can switch positions on the court, but the ones who started the serve in the front row are still considered the front-row players. A player can touch the floor across the center line with one or both feet or one or both hands as long as part of the foot or hand remains on or above the center line. But if a player interferes with play on the ball by the opposing team because a hand or foot is across the center line, then a line violation is called due to interference.

When blocking, blockers may reach over the net, but they cannot make contact with the ball until the other team makes the attack. You are not allowed to block a serve if a receiving team player at the net extends her arms in a blocking motion and the served ball touches her hands as it passes over the net. That's a violation on the receiving team and a point is awarded to the serving team. Hitters may cross the net only on their follow-through. If anyone touches the net at anytime, she loses the point.

If the ball touches the net on anything but the serve, it continues to be played. If it bounces back into the side of the team that was trying to send it over, the players may continue to hit it as long as: they don't use up their three hits; a player does not hit the ball twice in a row; and the ball doesn't first bounce from the net onto the floor. Play continues even when a player touches a nonplayable area, such as a team bench, the officials' table, or the bleachers as long as the player does not break the plane of the non-playable area.

Only front-row players may attack or block the ball from within the 3-meter line. In fact, the players who are in the front row can attack from anywhere on the court. Back-row players, on the other hand, cannot attack in the front area, which extends from the net to 3 meters back (about 10 feet). They can stand in front of this 3-meter line and touch the ball, but they are not allowed to hit it above the plane of the top of the net, even if it is not an attack. They are allowed a back-row attack, as long as the player doesn't take off in front of the line. She can jump from behind it and land in front of it, though, once the ball has been hit.

THOSE ARE THE RULES, BUT HOW DO YOU PLAY?

When volleyball was first played, the ball was slapped back and forth over the net until someone missed. Of course, teams that had good teamwork could put together a sequence that resulted in a good hit, but the finely tuned game plans of today didn't exist. For instance, while it is completely legal for a team to return the ball in one or two hits, this almost never happens. This is because taking advantage of all three hits has been proven to be more effective.

Each of the three hits has a function. These functions are called, in order, the FOREARM PASS (or DIG), the SET, and the SPIKE. The forearm pass is used to receive the serve and pass the ball up near the net; the set is a short controlled pass that places the ball in perfect position for attack; and the spike is the attack itself—usually toward the floor of the opposite court.

The three hits define the players' roles. Today it's extremely unlikely to have each player expecting to do any of the three hits. By specializing, players can concentrate on improving the skills that pertain to their own particular role and minimize the confusion over who is going to hit the ball.

Specialization is most apparent in the SETTER position. If one girl on a team is an expert setter, it would be advantageous for her team to allow her to do it for all the sets. In such cases, no matter where this setter is in the rotation, she moves up to the front center of the court as soon as the ball is served.

The same is true of expert hitters, spikers, diggers, and blockers. Coaches give their players specific roles, and they perform them (except where they are limited by the rules, such as a quick hitter being stuck in the back row) no matter where they are in the rotation.

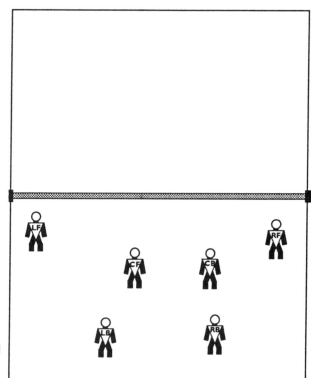

Wherever setter is in rotation, she moves up to front center of court as soon as ball is served. The quick hitters, good spikers, diggers, and blockers also change positions.

Mastering these nuances—and playing by the rules—is what makes competitive, power volleyball so much more challenging than its poor country cousin, the picnic volleyball game. Since volleyball has become such a strictly defined and popular sport in high school, girls finally face the level of competition that is worthy of being a precursor to top-notch volleyball.

2

TRAINING

The coach blows the whistle, which can only mean one thing—more sprinting! You groan quietly to yourself. "Line up on the end line!" the coach commands.

Do coaches use sprints as a form of torture to keep their players in line? Sometimes. Have they run out of more fun things to do at practice? Occasionally. Are these the real reasons why conditioning is such a vital part of volleyball training? Absolutely not. No one is going to be able to play volleyball well without being in top physical shape, and coaches know it.

A team whose players are less skilled but in good shape will beat a more skilled out-of-shape team every time. The latter team might score some points in the beginning, but soon it will be less aggressive on defense, slower on transition, and sloppier in passing, setting, and hitting. After a few tough losses, the team will wish it had done some more sprinting.

Getting in shape means more than just doing wind sprints. You have to build endurance and strength, hone skills, and increase flexibility. All of these are vital if you want to become a good volleyball player. And you don't have to wait for a coach to initiate training—do it yourself!

Volleyball is vigorous, and it's never too soon to start training your body to handle its demands. You must get yourself into shape by stretching and building your muscles, sprinting short and medium-length distances, and learning how to jump.

First, you have to make sure you're physically fit. Volleyball is mostly an anaerobic sport (not building heart and lung endurance), so the best training would be short burst drills. You should focus on very intensive exercise for a short period of time and then rest, because that is how volleyball is played. Unless you're going to be a SETTER, who runs all over the court, there's really no need to bother jogging. If you can run 2 miles with relative ease, then you are ready for the real training.

STRETCHING

Before beginning any training program or volleyball game, you need to stretch your muscles. But it's important for the muscles to be warm before you begin stretching. Run a few laps around the gym and set a few balls against the gymnasium wall before stretching out. It's safer, and you'll get more out of it.

Your whole body participates in the sport of volleyball, so you need to stretch all of the muscle groups. This is not an easy task. A good way to do it is to work from the feet up to the head, stretching each muscle for about a minute. This way it is unlikely that you will miss an important muscle group.

Stretching should feel good. If it doesn't, then you are probably doing something wrong. Keep your body relaxed and don't forget to breathe. Also, don't bounce or stretch to the point of pain.

Lower Leg

To start, rotate your ankles. Get them loosened up. Then work on your Achilles tendon and the backs of your calves. The best way to do this is to keep your feet flat on the floor and then walk your hands out until you feel your heels start to lift. Allow one heel to come up and keep the other one on the floor; you'll feel a good stretch up the back of your calf. This is called the mountain climber stretch. If you bend your knee on the leg you are stretching, you'll feel it in the Achilles tendon. After one leg is stretched well, switch and do the other leg. If you want to be tremendously efficient in your stretching, you can rotate the ankle of the leg that is not being stretched.

Quads and Hamstrings

To stretch the upper leg, stand up again. Lift one foot up behind you and grab the ankle. Now push your foot out until you feel a stretch down the front of your thigh. If you have trouble balancing, focus on a spot on the floor about 6 feet away. Switch and do the other leg.

To stretch the back of the thigh, cross one leg over the other and bend down to touch your toes. Then cross your legs the other way and stretch the other side.

The mountain climber stretch

The quad stretch

The hamstring stretch

Middle Body

The hip flexor runs from the top of your thigh to your trunk and happens to be a muscle that most people never get around to stretching. To isolate it, get in a sprinter's crouch with your hands on the floor. Then extend the back leg out as far as it can go and press your hip toward the ground. The stretch you feel is the hip flexor.

Now it's an easy transition into an inner thigh and groin stretch. Rotate your body toward your back leg. That back leg will go from being supported by the toes to being supported by the heel. You should

The hip flexor stretch

The inner thigh stretch

The pretzel stretch for your outer leg and hip

The butterfly stretch for your groin

The waist stretch

The shoulder stretch

The triceps stretch

now feel the stretch in your inner thigh. Switch legs and do both the hip flexor and the inner thigh stretch again.

To stretch the outside of the hips, use the pretzel stretch. Extend one leg out straight and bend the other one over it. Turn your body toward the hip of the bent leg. Press that knee into your body, and you should feel the stretch in the hip. Switch and do the other leg.

To stretch the groin, the butterfly stretch is good. Sit on the floor and touch the soles of your feet together. Bring your feet close in toward your body, and at the same time try to press your knees down to the ground. Some people prefer to leave their feet out and then lean over, while pressing their knees down.

Finally, to stretch your waist and sides, sit back up and spread your legs. Lean to one side and try to make your ear parallel to the ground. Bring your arm up over your head, keeping that in line with the ear as well. Do not lean forward.

Arms

To stretch the shoulders, bring one arm straight across the body. Pull the forearm back, keeping the elbow stiff, until you feel the stretch. Do this with the other arm.

The back of the arm, or triceps muscle, is another good muscle to stretch. Raise the arm, bend the elbow, and then try to move the elbow behind the head. Repeat this with the other arm.

RUNNING

Sprints

Once you are stretched, it's time for what is known as short burst training. Sixty- or 80-yard sprints are the most effective. Run one sprint every 60 or 90 seconds, depending on the distance. The faster you run, the longer your rest period. Start off by doing two sets of eight and run at 80 to 90 percent speed. Every time you run eight sprints, take a two-minute break.

In sprint training, you don't want to be winded when you go again. You'll get much more out of it if you rest the full minute and are fresh for the next sprint. Increase to three and then four sets of eight over the next few weeks. If you can do that, you'll be in good shape.

Touch-and-Go Sprints

Because volleyball is full of short, sharp cuts in many directions, sprint exercises nicknamed "touch and gos" are especially effective. If your

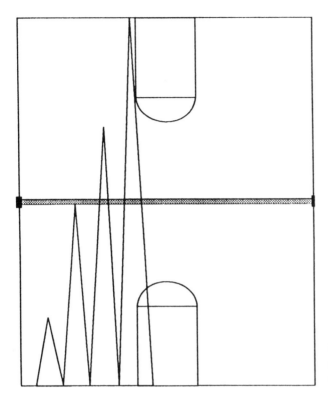

**Touch-and-go drill
for basketball and
volleyball courts**

volleyball courts are in a gym where basketball is played, you can use those court markings; otherwise use the volleyball court markings or mark out the running area on your own.

Begin your touch and go at the baseline and sprint to the basketball foul line. Make a quick turn, sprint back to the baseline, another quick turn, and down to the half-court line. Turn again, back to the baseline, then the far foul line, back, and then the end line and back. This will train your body to handle the type of movement that volleyball requires.

If you run these sprints on the volleyball court, the sprint is shorter, so just run more of them. Use the end lines, the 3-meter lines, and the center line.

Conditioners

Beyond mere sprinting is a level of training called conditioners. The idea of conditioners is to combine straight sprinting with other challenging body exercises. This, even more so than the other sprints, simulates the action in a real volleyball game, where you have to do many other things besides just sprinting.

For instance, begin your conditioner with a sprint from one end of the gym to the other and back again. As soon as you're back at the starting line, do an exercise, such as push-ups, for 30 seconds. Now jog to the end of the gym and back. Rest for 30 seconds, and begin the cycle again with a new exercise.

There are many good exercises to do between the sprints of a conditioner. Here are just a few:

1. sit-ups
2. jumping jacks
3. line leaps (jumping back and forth over a line on the court with both feet)
4. mountain climbers (propping your body up with your hands while your feet simulate a climbing motion)
5. ski tucks (jumping and bringing your knees to your chest each time)

Practicing your jump timing should be a part of training

JUMPING

A talented jumper can have a tremendous advantage in volleyball, yet many players neglect this aspect of their workout. Leg strength is crucial to a good jump, and there are a number of ways to increase it.

You also should work on your jump timing, which can be just as important a skill as setting or serving. Stand in front of a net and have someone toss balls from the other side as you jump up to block them. When you feel comfortable with that, increase the pace to a more gamelike situation, with serves, hits, and spikes. Your aim is to block them all.

Stairs

Stairs are a jumper's best friend. Every time you go up or down stairs, you are working on your quadriceps. Increase the challenge and you'll increase the workout. You can either sprint up and walk down or do two-footed hops every second or third step.

Wall Jumping

Clearly, leg strength is vital to good jumping, but practicing the art of jumping is important too. Stand next to a wall with a piece of chalk in your hand. Hold it up high and leap into the air, leaving a chalk mark on the wall as high up as you can get. Now do 20 jumps for that mark. Make sure that every one of them is at or above your chalk mark.

Cone Jumping

A great jumping drill for your whole team involves about 10 cones lined up in a row about 1 foot apart. Players should line up and then proceed through the row of cones, using two-footed jumps over each cone.

To begin with, you should move through the row jumping straight ahead. Next you should go through jumping sideways to the right. After that go through jumping sideways to the left. The last time through, alternate jumping forward and jumping sideways. This helps build strength, endurance, jumping skills, and the ability to change directions quickly.

WEIGHTS

Many schools have weight machines. Though these can be tremendously helpful for building strength, they are not meant for everyone. If you haven't reached your full height yet, then weight training will

Jumping forward over cones

Jumping sideways over cones

do more harm than good. Unless you wait until your muscles are developed, you'll damage them by using weights.

If you've had your growth spurt, then weight training can help you to become a more effective volleyball player. If you are new to weight training, you should do isolated exercises, such as those with Nautilus equipment. The machines isolate your muscle groups and can be used to develop strength in specific weak muscle groups. Keep in mind, however, that technique is very important. For instance, if you use a stationary bicycle, you should make sure to keep your knees bent in order to isolate your quadriceps muscles. You should always work with a coach or a trainer when you do weight training, so you will be aware of important special instructions.

MENTAL TRAINING

Your mind's fitness also plays a large role in whether your body is ready to play volleyball or not. Concentration is the key. During a game, you have to be alert and aware at all times. You're going to have to anticipate the moves of your own teammates as well as guess the trickier bluffs and moves of your opponents.

Players often make mistakes because their minds aren't totally in the game. They don't recover from a break or their mind drifts back to something they should have done. A wandering mind accounts for more errors than you could possibly imagine.

PLAY TIME

After all is said and done, the best way to get both your mind and body in shape is to play. And that means *serious* play. You want to get to game speed and under gamelike conditions, not casual picnic volleyball. Train the way you want to play. If you want to play hard, aggressive, and smart, that's the way you want to train.

Good volleyball play will exercise not only your muscles but your brain as well. You have to learn to deal with the pressures, the anxieties, the fears, and all the emotions that you experience in a game. You might think you have a skill down pat, but if you haven't practiced it under pressure, there's no guarantee you will remember it when you are in a tough game situation.

When you're concentrating on a million mental aspects of the game, your physical ability has to be second nature. This means that your practices must include some competition. You need to practice competing and coping with pressure just as much as you must practice the physical mechanics of playing.

DRILLS

1. All good volleyball players possess two characteristics: agility and leg strength. This drill helps build both.

From the passing stance, shuffle to the left and right to develop balance, quickness, and agility. Keep your feet pointed out and don't cross them.

Three players line up an equal distance apart along the midline of the court. Each player gets in a passing stance—feet slightly further than shoulder-width apart, toes pointing forward, body bent at the waist. On the coach's signal, players take shuffle steps—moving laterally without crossing the feet—to their right approximately 4 feet. Make sure to straddle the lines (as shown). Then shuffle step back to the middle and continue 4 feet to the left, again straddling the lines.

Repeat this for 30 seconds. The key to this drill is making sure that players stay down in their stance and don't turn their feet out to the side. Don't let them cross their feet!

2. This is a great conditioning drill, but it also helps players develop a "net sense."

Have the front row players pair up, facing one another on opposite sides of the net. On the coach's signal, the players jump up and touch each other's hands over the top of the net. Make sure that they do not touch the net on the way up or down.

Start out with 20 touches and work up to sets of 40. A way to revise this drill is to make it mandatory to complete a certain number of touches within a specified amount of time.

3. This drill is borrowed from the sport of football, and it helps players lose their fear of dropping to the floor. Dropping to the floor and diving are essential movements for good defense.

   Players run in place, arms held out in front of them. The coach points in a particular direction and the players quickly turn and face that way. When the coach says, "Hit the deck!," the players hit the floor and bounce back up.

   By practicing this drill, players become comfortable with the act of dropping to the floor, so they won't hesitate to do it during match play.

4. This relay race is a great way to end your practice. It's a conditioning drill that forces players to concentrate on a variety of volleyball skills.

   Two coaches are needed for this drill. Divide the team into two squads. Have both teams line up on the same end of the court in a single-file line. One team stands on the left side of the court, the other stands on the right side, and each player has a ball.

   The race begins with the first player in line hitting an overhand serve to her side of the court. The serve must be in play for the player to advance. If the ball lands out of play or hits the net, the player must serve again until the ball lands in play. After the serve, the player sprints to the front of the net. She stops, hits the deck, runs under the net, and sprints to the opposite end of the court. She turns around and the coach tosses her a ball. She must forearm pass the ball back to the other end of the court. She then sprints to the net, drops to the floor, and sprints back to the line where she then slaps the hand of her teammate. The next person starts. The first team to finish wins the race.

3
THE SERVE

A slight toss of the ball and then the arm comes whistling forward, sending the volleyball across the net and into the back corner of the court with almost no spin. Will it go out of bounds, or will it be good? At the last second, the opponents realize it's going to be in bounds, and they dive for the ball. But they aren't quite quick enough. The serve scores!

Every volley in a volleyball game begins with a serve. It's how the ball is put into play. But a serve can be executed in three very distinct styles: the OVERHEAD FLOAT SERVE, the JUMP SERVE, and the UNDERHAND SERVE. The overhead float serve is the most popular, as it's a strong serve that is fairly easy to master. The jump serve is relatively new but is rapidly gaining ground; it's more difficult, but can be a powerful weapon once it is mastered. The underhand serve is for younger players and picnic volleyball players. It doesn't require as much strength and is easy to learn, but it is not very effective in scoring points. No matter which serve a player chooses, however, she will have to follow the same serve restrictions.

The ball must be served from behind the END LINE and within the designated 3 meters that are marked off on the right side of the court. There is no restriction, however, as to how far back you can go. As long as you're between the serving markers and behind the end line, you can go as far backwards as you want. You get only *one chance* to get the ball in play, so your primary responsibility is accuracy. Anything that helps you should become a permanent part of your serve routine.

The tricky part is then developing a serve that will get you points. You can't just master the motion, you need to develop serving strategy. For instance, most beginning volleyball players place the ball in the center of the court, right into the waiting arms of a receiver. Instead,

The overhead serve

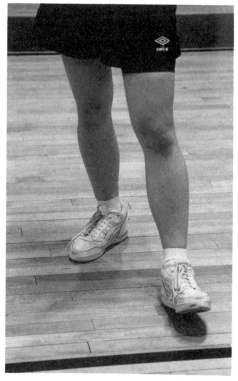

The overhead serving stance

you want to practice serving into an open space or to a spot where it's uncertain as to who will handle the ball. Receivers pass a ball better when they don't have to move, so you want to make it difficult for them by making them move.

In other words, you have to do more than just get the ball into play. With a good serve, you help your team in two ways. First, there's the chance that you may get an ACE, which gives your team the point right away. Even if your opponents manage to get their hands on the ball, a tough serve will make it difficult for them to mount a strong offensive move. When the ball comes back weakly over the net, your team can put it away for a point.

THE OVERHEAD FLOAT SERVE

Ninety percent of the people who play volleyball use the overhead floater serve. It's not too difficult to learn, and it's effective because there's a lot of force behind it.

The toss

The Stance

Before you begin any serve, establish your starting stance. Begin in a stride position. If you're right-handed, your left foot should be forward, and your right foot is behind. Most of your weight should be on that back right foot.

Both of your feet should be pointed to the other side of the court, not off to the side. Some players prefer to point their feet exactly toward the area they are targeting, although doing so may signal your intent to the opponent.

The Toss

Once you've established the stance, you have to remember only three steps: toss, step, hit. If you're a right-handed server, the toss will come from your left hand (and vice versa). You'll want to hold the ball up around shoulder level. If you look forward, you should just be able to see over the top of the ball. The arm is bent a comfortable distance away from the body and lined up with the hitting shoulder; it should be a straight line from hitting arm to ball to target.

The toss is the most critical part of the serve. If you can keep it consistently in the same place, then your hitting motion can always be the same, which is the key to accurate serves. That way, any change in your hitting motion is purely to direct the ball. If you have to change your hitting motion because of a bad toss, you'll have no opportunity to direct the ball where you want it to go.

Moving your whole arm, loft the ball to a height between 12 and 18 inches. You'll have to figure out the height that works best for you, because the ball should be waiting in the air, just as your hand is coming through to hit it. If your toss is too high, you'll have to halt your arm swing, and you'll lose all of the momentum and power. If the toss is too low, you'll have to rush the arm swing, and you won't have the full, fluid, extended motion, which could cause control problems.

Keep the tossing hand stiff at the wrist as you release the ball. It's not a hand toss; it's an *arm* toss. Keep the ball out in front. If a perfect toss is dropped to the ground, it would hit the big toe of your stepping foot after the step.

The Hit

Then it's time to put it all together. As you toss the ball, the weight is on your back foot. As your arm comes through to hit the ball, shift your weight forward, without taking a step, so when the serve is over, all your weight is on the front foot.

Before the toss, most people like to rest their hitting arm on top of the volleyball, but as the toss goes up, the elbow bends and the arm is drawn back. As you begin the hit, your elbow is completely bent and your hitting arm is shoulder height or above. And, like the tossing arm, the wrist on the hitting arm is stiff. This will help create the floater aspect of the serve.

The serving action is very much like throwing. You start with the elbow back and then you bring your arm forward to the ball with your shoulders, elbows, hips, and the rest of the body following. This should

(Above and next page) Putting the overhead serve together

all be done very quickly, however, to get the most power
out the body movement.

When you contact the ball,
you want it to be as far out in
front of you as you can toler-
ate and still have control. The
contact is a punching-type
action with the meaty part of
your hand in the center of the
ball. If you do it correctly, the
effect will be a floater or a
knuckleball type of ball with
very little spin. Without spin,
the ball tends to wiggle in the
air, making it very hard to follow—and that's the idea of the
serve.

Center contact is the key
to the floater serve. If you hit
the ball too low, you'll get
underspin; if you hit the side,

The contact point

you'll get sidespin; and if you snap your wrist, you'll get topspin. Keeping the wrist firm and hitting the ball straight on is very important.

THE JUMP SERVE

The jump serve is much more difficult than the overhead serve, but
the extra speed and power it generates is incentive enough for many
players to attempt to develop a good one. The jump serve started to
appear on the volleyball scene in the late 1970s and early '80s, performed mostly by Brazilians and other South Americans, but it didn't
really gain total acceptance until the 1984 Olympics.

The jump serve evolved from a reinterpretation of the serving
restrictions, and it takes advantage of the flexibility of movement
behind the end line. To begin with, jump servers have to get a good
start for their jump, so they begin well behind the line. In addition,
they take advantage of the fact that the rule of not crossing the end
line pertains only to the time when your feet are on the ground. If you
toss the ball in the air, you can hit it while you are above the line in
the air, and then land inside the court. Essentially, what you want to
do with a jump serve is broad jump into the court, getting yourself as
close to the net as you can with as much power as possible.

The jump serve

A two-handed toss

The jump serve is quite legal—and it can be very effective against teams that use only two people to receive serves. Most teams will bring in a third person if the opponents do a lot of jump serves.

Currently, because it is newer, the jump serve is not used as much as the float serve, although that will probably change. Already, almost every beach volleyball player can do a jump serve. Even so, since only about 10 percent of high school girls can use jump serves effectively right now, spending the time to develop such serves is probably not worthwhile.

The Toss

There are two methods of tossing: two hands or one hand. If you use two hands, the toss looks like an underhand flip, but a fairly strong one. If you use one hand, you toss with your nonhitting hand, just as in the overhead serve. Either way, you want to toss the ball about 5 to 6 feet in the air—high enough so you can run, jump, and meet it at your highest point.

(Above) The bow-and-arrow position for the jump serve

(Above and on next page) Putting the jump serve together

The Steps

It's important to use the exact same running and jumping motion on every serve, so you can time your hit perfectly. You'll need to know whether to use one, two, or three steps. Most people tend to use the two-step approach. You toss the ball up, take a step with your right foot (assuming you are hitting with your right hand), and plant with your left foot. Your plant should be a strong step to boost your body into the air.

The Hit

The best way to describe the jump serve hit is to say it resembles the motions of an archer. You want make a bow and arrow with your arms by bringing the elbow of your hitting arm all the way back—so that your hand is by your ear—and extending your other arm all the way out in front for balance and extra momentum.

To hit, you want to straighten your elbow and snap through the ball as if you were SPIKING, which is described in Chapter 6. As your arm comes through, the motion becomes more like throwing a baseball than shooting a bow and arrow. As your shoulder comes forward with the hitting arm, your hips and the rest of your body follow. This motion creates topspin.

THE UNDERHAND SERVE

The underhand serve is basically a desperation serve or a casual player's serve. It falls into the court in a slow lob, giving the other team plenty of time to react and mount an aggressive attack. It should be used only by girls who do not

The underhand serve

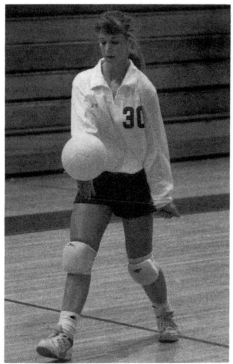

(This page and next) Putting the underhand serve together

have the physical strength or haven't yet had the opportunity to develop a good overhead serve.

An easy test to determine sufficient strength is to have the player stand on the end line and try to throw the ball over the net as deep into the court as possible. If she can't do that, then she is too weak and should use the underhand serve. But if she can get the ball over by throwing, start her working on the proper motion for the overhead immediately. Her problems probably just stem from poor mechanics.

The Stance

To execute the underhand serve, you should stand in the same stride position as for the overhead serve. Again, if you're right-handed, your left foot is forward and your right foot is behind, bearing your weight.

The Hit

Hold the ball in your nonhitting hand. Think of this hand as a golf tee or a T-ball stand, which allows the ball to be perched up perfectly still.

Your hitting hand should be cocked back, with the fist clenched to form a flat surface. Swing through in a pendulum-type fashion toward the target, keeping your elbow straight. Stride forward and shift your weight from the right foot to the left foot.

PRACTICING

The best way to practice any serve is to concentrate on one aspect, while performing the entire motion. If you can do this, you get the idea of what a serve feels like and looks like as a whole. If, however, you take the serve apart and practice the separate pieces, putting it all together again into one smooth serving motion is very hard.

For instance, if you want to develop a good arm toss, you might be tempted to just toss the ball up 50 times. Instead, however, you should do 50 serves, with the toss as the focus of your concentration. Then you might concentrate on shifting your body weight forward as you hit the ball or practice swinging through your target. No matter what, you should do the entire serve every time.

THE CHANGE-UP

The ideal situation for a volleyball player is to keep the opponents off guard by alternating between overhead and jump serves. But that's not often possible, especially at the high school level. If it's not likely that you will be able to master the jump serve, you might want to try developing the CHANGE-UP.

The trick with any change-up—whether it's in volleyball or baseball—is masking your intentions. The delivery should look the same whether the ball's going deep or short, fast or slow. As the server, you want to use the same motion, so your opponents can't predict what type of ball it's going to be just from looking at you. The only change you might want to make is for a short ball; in this case, toss the ball a little nearer in order to give it a slight lob to get it over the net.

If you're having trouble developing your change-up, you may want to move a good distance back behind the end line. You can hit the ball hard every time. The ball will vary itself—short, long, short—and it will go at about the same speed no matter where it lands, so the receiver won't be able to key on it.

STRATEGY

Many new volleyball players worry only about getting the serve over the net and into the court, but a good serve involves a lot more. Once you become more skilled, you should learn to place the ball where you want.

If one receiver is weaker than the other, hit it to the weak one every time. Sometimes a player may not be weaker initially, but the game situation might turn her into a weaker player. For instance, if she just made a mistake, she might be flustered. Serve to her. If she has been distracted by the coach or the crowd, or has just argued with the referee, she might not have her head fully in the game. Serve to her. Anyone who has just subbed in is also a perfect target. Chances are she'll be cold and won't have picked up the momentum yet. Serve to her.

Another objective for a server is to identify what kind of serve gives the whole opposing team the most difficulty. On many teams, receivers are responsible for covering a huge distance, from the short-serve area around the net all the way to the end line. Being able to pinpoint serves either short or deep is a great advantage. It keeps the receivers off balance, so they don't know what to expect and can't cheat in one direction.

If you do your homework, you can discover which direction—up, back, left, or right—gives the opposing team the most difficulty, and then you should place the ball there. For instance, if someone has trou-

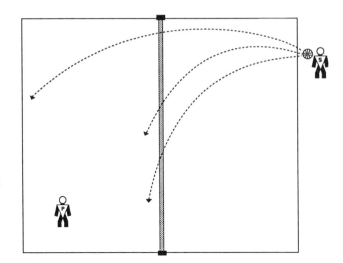

If a digger has trouble moving forward, your serve distribution should be two short, one deep, two short, one deep.

ble moving forward, then your serve distribution should be two short, one deep, two short, one deep; thus when the match is over, two-thirds of the serves would have been served short, which gives the player problems, and one-third would have been served deep, to keep the player honest.

It's important to remember, however, that your primary responsibility is to get the ball into the court. Don't play around with your serve so much that you end up missing the court entirely.

Because of their inexperience, high school players often miss serves at the wrong time. Sometimes players try a fancy serve after they've won a few points in a row; in fact, at this time they should be doing just the opposite. If you've just served 5 points, then you don't want to try a low-percentage serve. Just get the ball into the court the way you have been, because the opposition is having problems already. But suppose your opponents have SIDED OUT—prevented your team from getting a point—10 times in a row. They're in a good rhythm and there's a strong chance that they'll side out again. Then you have nothing to lose by trying a risky serve. It might throw the opposition off balance and be the key you need to start getting some points. Sometimes an ace is all that's needed to start up team momentum.

There are several rules of thumb to follow:

1. Never miss two serves in a row. If you missed the first time up, make sure you get the ball in play the second time around.
2. Keep up the momentum. If you're winning points, get the serves in the court.

3. If you are following a player who has just missed her serve, make certain to get yours in.
4. If you score several points in a row and the other team calls time out to disrupt your momentum, get your next serve in.

DRILLS

1. For basic serve mechanics, girls should pair up and have one ball for each pair. They stand opposite one another on either side of the net and just serve back and forth. Several pairs can fit on one court.
2. Practicing serve after serve can get a little boring. It's fun to turn a drill into a game. Players line up, each with a ball, on one side of the net. On the other side, mark a line about 4 feet (more or less, depending on the skill of the servers) in from the end line, the sidelines, and the net. This will form a square in the center of the court. If the ball drops outside the square, it's worth 1 point, and if it drops in the center, it's worth 0 points. The center is where most serves go, and they aren't very effective. If the serve goes out of the court entirely, it is minus 1 point. This not only makes the practice more interesting, but it helps teach serve placement.

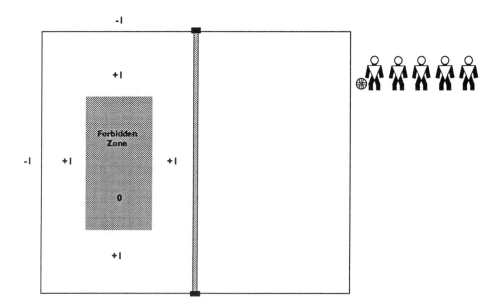

Drill 2, a ball outside square is worth 1 point, and in square it's 0 points. A serve out of court entirely is minus 1 point.

When serving, your weight must be forward to strike the ball. Use the meaty part of your hand to make contact.

3. This drill develops the skill of precision serving. You'll need a roll of white athletic tape and a paper and pencil to keep score. Use the tape to divide the court into equal parts—15 feet wide by 10 feet deep—on each side of the net. Divide the team into two, with half the players on one side of the net and half on the other. Have the players take turns serving the ball.

Each server is now looking at six boxes (15 feet wide by 10 feet long) into which they may serve the ball. The object is to land the ball in a specific box using an overhand serve. The coach can yell out short, middle, or deep box. Landing the ball in the deep box is worth two points, the middle box one point, and the short box three points. The short box requires a soft touch, and therefore it receives the highest score for this drill. The ball must land in the box specifically announced by the coach to receive any points. Each player gets 10 serves and tries to accumulate the most points.

Remember to keep your weight on your rear foot as you toss the ball up and to shift forward as your hand hits through the ball.

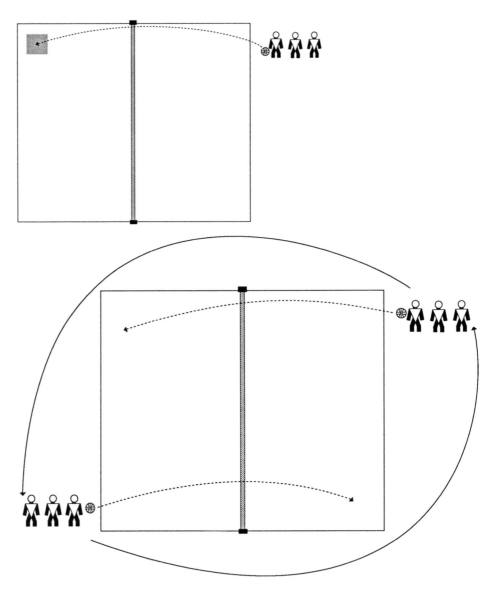

Drill 4, serve and receive. The two lines serve to open space in the opposite court. Use the meaty part of your hand to make contact.

4. In this drill, there are two lines on opposite sides of the net and every girl has a ball. Players serve, retrieve their own ball, and go to the end of the other line. The two lines are serving down the line to the open space in the opposite court, not crosscourt to the other line.

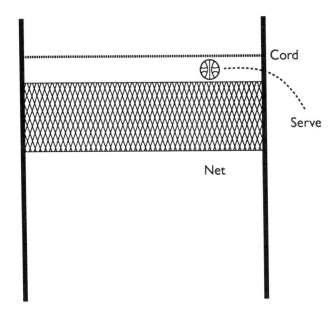

Drill 5, to develop flat-line serve, put a rope or cord about 2 feet above net.

5. To help players develop a serve that goes on a flat line, put a plastic cord about 2 feet above the net. Then have the girls try to serve underneath the cord. You can set up a competition by combining the last drill with this one. The line that is first to complete 10 successful, under-the-cord serves is the winner.

6. If you've ever played the game "horse" in basketball, this drill will seem familiar. One player, Server A, announces where she is going to serve—for example, the front right corner. If she places the ball in the area she designated, Server B has to repeat the exact same serve or Server A gets a point. If Server B makes it, then Server A has to repeat the same serve again until someone misses. At that point, the person who didn't miss gets the point and gets the opportunity to choose the next serve. If a player misses on the very first serve, the other player does not get a point, but the serve choice goes to her.

4

THE SERVE RECEIVE OR FOREARM PASS

United States volleyball teams were a little slow to incorporate the FOREARM PASS into their game plans. For years, the ball was always hit with both hands over the head. For a very low serve, the receivers would just crouch down even lower to get under it. This changed with the 1964 Olympics.

The U.S. Volleyball Team had been practicing nonstop, and it was ready to make an impression in the Tokyo Olympics. Team members had their serves down pat, their timing was flawless in their sets and hits, and they knew how to do the two-handed OVERHEAD PASS perfectly. And that was the problem. The U.S. Olympic team arrived in Japan only to be told that the overhead pass was not acceptable and the players had to use the forearm pass.

Team members stared in disbelief. They had no practice in the forearm pass at all! Needless to say, it was time for a crash course. Even though the team didn't win any gold medals to show for their effort, they did bring home a new skill. They loved the forearm pass, and the word spread to volleyball players across the country.

Today the forearm pass is one of the most common and important hits a volleyball player can use. It gives a player more reaction time and can be executed in a wide variety of situations, including SERVE RECEIVE, DIGGING, SETTING, handling a low ball in a rally, or passing during transition. But the most common situation is during the serve receive, and that's where the focus should begin.

The objective of the serve receive is to send the ball in a nice high arc to the SETTER spot. If the ball is high and close to the net, the setter has all her options open—forward, backward, or a quick hit. A bad pass might mean that she can set only to the player in front of her. The defense will have no trouble keying on her.

The serve receive is anything but easy. Although it sounds simple, it's very important for the pass to be completely accurate. Usually serves are coming in hard and fast and in a spot where you aren't, so it's hard to gain control of them.

THE LEGS

To be a good serve receiver, you have to be able to move forward, backward, and side to side. While a lot of this depends on natural ability and quickness, there are some steps any girl can take to make herself faster in order to beat a ball to a spot.

Standing in a stride position is the first key. If your feet are parallel, you're going to move much slower—especially forward and back-

The forearm pass

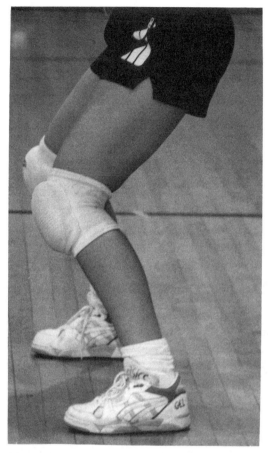

The ready position, one leg in front of the other

ward. Keep in mind that this tip works for both defense and offense. If you see receivers on the other team standing with their feet parallel, try to place your hits short or deep, rather than left or right. Players with parallel feet lose forward/backward mobility.

While you can put either foot forward, most people—both righties and lefties—prefer to have their left foot forward. It shouldn't be too far forward, though. The big toe of one foot should be just about parallel to the heel of the other foot. Your feet should be shoulder width apart and comfortable. Your knees should be bent enough to extend out in front over your toes.

Once you are in stride position, there are two different ways to move. The first is the SHUFFLE STEP. Use this motion when you don't have to go far and when the ball is moving slowly. To shuffle to the right, for instance, slide the left foot over to the right and then take a step with the right foot. Then slide the left foot over again, and so on. These two foot movements should be happening very quickly and almost simultaneously.

The second way to move is called a CROSSOVER move. If a ball is not heading near you and is traveling at a fast pace, a shuffle step will not get you to it in time. You're going to have to do a crossover, which is more like running. Again, imagine you are going to the right. You cross the left foot over the right and then take a step with the right. With the crossover, you cover a much longer distance with each step.

THE ARMS

Now that leg movement is established, you have to begin the pass itself. Your arms should be relaxed. You don't want to be stiff. Hold your arms up in a medium-high position, ready to hit the ball. Because you won't have time to get them up into position once the ball is served, you must start out this way.

This "ready" position is referred to as a PLATFORM, and it's the most important part of the pass. The ball will bounce off the platform. To create it, bring your arms together. Open them up, so that the fleshy underside of the arm (the part that never gets tan) is facing upward. Now bring the elbows in close together, keeping the arms parallel. This widens the hitting area. The ideal place to connect with the volleyball is the sweet spot, about 4 inches in from the hands. You can be off an inch or two either way, but you don't want to hit the ball with your wrists because they're too bumpy, and you don't want to hit the ball too far back, because you might end up double hitting it.

THE GRIP

It's easy enough to make the platform with your arms when the ball is nowhere in the vicinity, but once that volleyball hits your forearm, you better have a great grip or your platform is going to look like two sides of the San Andreas fault. In other words, rather than rebounding off your platform, the ball will go through your arms to the floor.

In addition to bringing your arms together to form a platform, you also must hold them together with your hands. When the pass is over, your hands should still be held together.

There are a few different types of grips. The most popular is the interlocking grip. This is when all the fingers are interlaced, like a couple holding hands. The thumbs do not interlock, however, and they're placed side by side. It's a strong grip, but its biggest drawback is that, with it, jamming your fingers is a real possibility if you try to go for a ball near the floor.

Another method is the scoop method, in which you lay one hand, facing up, in the palm of the other. The thumb of the bottom hand wraps around the fingers of the top to make the grip tight. While this decreases the risk of finger jamming, the scoop is a less secure grip than the interlocking one.

The third method is to make a fist with one hand and wrap the other hand around it. Again, the thumbs are aligned side by side. The disadvantage here is that it is very hard to make this grip a strong one and still turn the fleshy part of the forearm up.

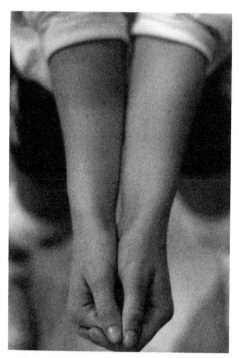

Form a platform with your forearms by bringing your elbows together

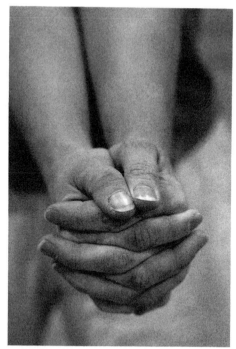

The interlocking grip

The scoop grip

The fist grip

If you're not sure which grip is best for you, try all of them or create your own. The keys to remember, however, are that you want something strong enough to withstand a powerful serve, and you want to be able to bring your elbows close together.

ON THE RIGHT TRACK

Now that you've gotten the legs, the arms, and the hands set for a forearm pass, what next? You just have to wait for the serve. Your head should be up watching the incoming serve, and your eyes should be on the ball. Keep your body movements to a minimum. You wouldn't want to be swaying one way as the serve comes another. In volleyball, every millisecond is precious.

Once your legs get you into position, do not move them any more. Don't bounce and shuffle or let them give you any extra power. The rest of the pass can be—and should be!—executed perfectly with just the arms and shoulders.

When you finally make contact with the ball, play it at your waist and as far out in front of you as possible. This position will give you maximum control in where you send the ball.

SENDING THE BALL

In volleyball, there are basically two directions—horizontal and vertical—and everything else is a permutation. When you send the ball to the setter, all you have to worry about is how far to move your arms in each direction.

If you want the ball to go predominantly horizontally, contact it with your arms down. If you want it to go vertically, bring your arms up as you hit the ball. An easy way to understand this is to make your forearms face the direction of the pass. If you want to pass up to the ceiling, your forearms should face up. If you want to pass to the wall, your forearms should face that direction.

Of course, nobody wants to send the ball to the ceiling or to the wall. Horizontal and vertical by themselves are completely undesirable directions in volleyball; you need to practice to see which blend of the two results will send the ball in a high arc to the setter. You also must consider that the ball is not going to come to you at the same height every time, and you will need to practice every angle at every height until you get the exact same perfect forearm pass every time.

The angle is not the only aspect of the forearm pass that must be perfected. You also have to judge the amount of power you are going to put behind the ball. Much of this depends on the speed of the ball hit to you.

Arms are in a mostly vertical position in order to pass the ball on a mostly horizontal line

Arms are in a mostly horizontal position in order to pass the ball on a mostly vertical line

If it's a slow-moving ball, you'll have to give it a more vigorous swing because it won't rebound as well as a faster-moving ball. To make adjustments for a fast-moving ball, you should open your arms a little and let the ball push them into your body, which takes a lot of the force and energy off the ball.

Passing takes hours of practice, but it can be the difference between a good volleyball team and a bad one. The goal of the receiver is to make the setter's job easier; if the arc the ball follows is the same each time, the setter will know what to expect and can exercise all her options.

SERVE-RECEIVING STRATEGY

In addition to forearm practice, there are also some tactical things to think about. In the ideal situation, you know exactly what to do if you have control of the ball. You send a perfect pass up to the setter spot. Suppose, however, the other team has a great server and she prevents you from getting into a good passing position because the ball is hit practically out of reach. You won't be able to set up a perfect pass. To compensate, focus on just passing the ball high to make sure the setter will have time to move underneath it no matter where it goes.

The other aspect you need to pay attention to is your setter's position. If she is in the front row at the start of the serve, then you can give her a faster, more horizontal pass. But if she is starting in the back row, then you have to pass the ball high to give her a chance to move forward.

THE DIG

The DIG is a type of forearm pass that is used to counteract the SPIKE. Because the dig is such an important part of individual defense, aspects of it also are explained in Chapter 9. Nonetheless, it still falls under the category of a forearm pass, so its role and basic techniques are described briefly in this chapter.

In relation to the offense, the dig is used essentially at the same part of the sequence as the serve receive—as the "pass" in the pass-set-hit sequence. It's considerably more difficult to turn a spike than a serve receive into a good pass.

Consider the easier situation, the serve receive, in which the serve is coming over the net essentially on a horizontal line. Since it travels from the back of one side of the court to the back of the other side, there's a fair amount of time to react and get into position. Not so with the spike.

The spike, also called the attack, is a fast-moving bullet of a ball that usually is heading over the net and straight for the floor. The player who has hit the ball is most often up close to the net. This adds up to a powerful hit that leaves the defenders with almost no time to react. That's where the dig comes in.

Every player who is not blocking should be prepared to dig the spike. The first thing to do is get into the stride position that is normal for forearm passing. However, this time you put forward the foot closest to the sideline, no matter what feels most comfortable. You should face in toward the court because you probably won't have much time to react when the spike comes over the net.

Give yourself every extra millisecond to get into a good passing position. Stay low so you can contact the ball as near to the floor as possible. Keep your arms out, and get up on the balls of your feet so you can move in any direction immediately.

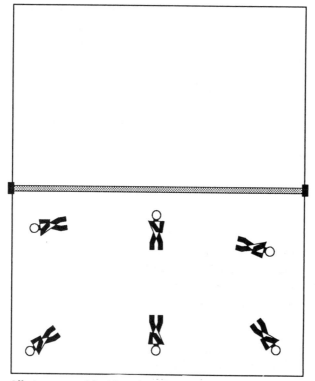

All players not blocking should prepare to dig spikes.

Once you are in position, the speed of the ball actually can work to your advantage. You won't have to swing your arms much at all to make the ball rebound high. In fact, sometimes you have to do the opposite and let your arms give a little to cushion the attack and reduce the velocity. Again, like the serve receive, the goal in the dig is to give the setter a nice high pass right to the setter spot.

NET SAVES

A NET SAVE is another use for the forearm pass. Even though the mechanics are the same, the two are considerably different. In the first place, net saves are usually done by the setter, because most often the pass from the serve receiver to the setter ends up unintentionally going into the net. Therefore, while this may be a good topic to cover in Chapter 5 on the set, it's here because the forearm pass is the best way to handle this type of situation.

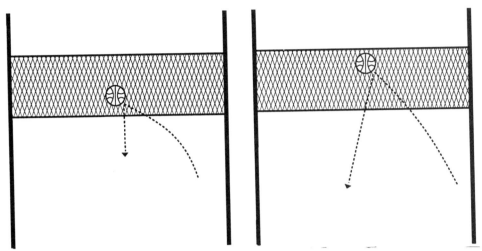

Ball hitting bottom of net usually catches and falls softly straight down.

Ball hitting top cord of net will go very fast and shoot straight down.

The ball reacts differently depending on where it hits on the net. If the ball hits at the bottom, it usually catches and softly falls straight down. To save it, face either the net or the sideline, and get low to the ground. Play the ball as close to the floor as possible, to give yourself more time to make a good pass. The net save should use the exact same mechanics as the forearm pass and bring the ball back into the court and high in the air.

If the ball hits at the top cord of the net, reacting is a lot harder. The ball will go very fast and shoot straight down. You must react quickly and anticipate the angles. If it's heading to the right, it will rebound to the right as well. If it's heading to the left, it will continue to go left. It will not rebound back. In either case, the ball will move in a downward angle, and it will be going fast. Simply do the best you can. Try to hit it high and bring it back and away from the net.

DRILLS

1. This is a very simple drill, used to focus entirely on forearm passing mechanics. Players divide into three groups of three and line up along the net. In each group of three there is a tosser, a passer, and a catcher. There are two balls for every group of three: one for the catcher and one for the tosser.

    The tosser stands on the other side and throws the ball over the net, varying the speed and location of her tosses. The passer makes

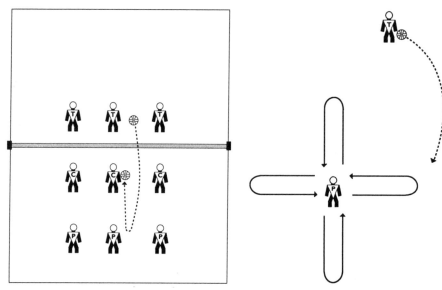

Drill 1, an exercise focusing on forearm passing mechanics

Drill 2, shuffle/crossover step

a beautifully executed pass up to the catcher, who then bounces the ball back to the tosser. They should go through about 15 repetitions and then rotate positions.

Keep in mind that two balls are going at once. The idea is to have the girls get in shape at the same time they're learning a skill. As soon as the tosser throws the first ball, the catcher should pass her the second one. To get a worthwhile workout, players should be moving all the time. With two balls you can minimize the rest period and maximize the repetitions in a short time.

Another nice aspect of this drill is that it allows players to concentrate on the fundamentals. And you can change its focus. First you might work on getting the legwork right. Then, after everyone rotates through each position, you can concentrate on facing the ball. The drill is the same but the emphasis changes.

2. This is a great drill for developing a good shuffle step or crossover step. Players should get into pairs—tosser and passer—with one ball. The passer stands on an X or a designated area on the floor. The tosser throws the ball toward the passer but to the left, right, forward, and behind the X and in no special pattern. No matter where the ball goes, the passer should get underneath it and send it right back to the tosser. After each toss, she should move back to X.

For very experienced players, the difficulty level can be increased by having two passers and no tosser. In this case, there is no X to stand on. The players just pass back and forth as if they were playing catch, but the whole time they're making forearm passes. They really have to stay focused in order to figure out where to go and then where to send the next ball. It's just like playing the game, so it's a great way to practice.

3. Because it's good for practice situations to be as realistic as possible, passers should work on receiving actual serves once they have the mechanics down pat. This a good drill for eight people. On each side of the net, there are two players, one server, and a target. The servers serve, while the receivers get the serve and pass to the target. The target catches the ball and tosses it to the server. The players keep these positions for a specified time or for a certain number of serves and then mix it up.

4. This drill forces you to focus on accurate forearm passing. Forearm passing is the most important link in setting up kill shots and spikes. If your pass to the setter is inaccurate, the final kill shot is in jeopardy. You need a coach and two players for this drill.

    The coach tosses the ball underhand over the net to a player stationed at the left back position. She receives the ball and sends a

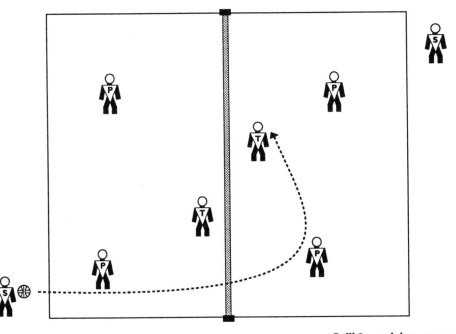

Drill 3, receiving serves

Direct your pass toward your teammate standing on the right side of the net. After delivering the pass, quickly run to the left side of the net to position yourself for the kill shot.

forearm pass to a player stationed at the right forward position. After advancing the pass, the left back runs forward to the net. The right forward sets the ball to the left back, who then leaps up to finish off a kill shot.

Remember: the receiver must focus on sending an accurate forearm pass to the setter. If she fails to do so, the play breaks down and a chance to score may be lost.

5. The last forearm passing drill is called the butterfly, and it's great for endurance and concentration in addition to developing forearm pass skills. It also forces players to try every position. Many teams like to use it as a warm-up drill, because it looks sharp and it gets everyone thinking and moving quickly.

The butterfly should be done in two groups of three, each group having a server, a passer, and a target, standing on the opposite sides of the net. As in the previous drill, the server hits the ball to the passer, who passes the ball to the target, who gives it to the

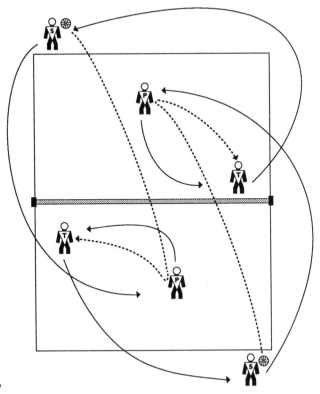

Drill 5, butterfly

server. However, in this drill, after serving, the server runs and takes the position of the opposite side passer. Accordingly, after passing, the passer moves to the target spot and the target moves to the serve position.

5
THE SET OR TWO-HAND OVERHEAD PASS

The SETTER on a volleyball team is akin to a pitcher on a softball team, the point guard on a basketball team, or the quarterback on a football team. The setter is the playmaker. Not only should she be smart, she also should be an expert at the two-hand overhead pass, otherwise known as the SET.

The set is usually the second of the three hits that are allowed per side. Its objective is to place the ball in a position that permits the hitter to get a good swing at it. It is called a set because the hit is so controlled that it's almost as if the ball were set up in the air on a little perch, like the baseball in a T-ball league.

THE HANDS AND ARMS

To execute the set, you first have to focus on using the hands properly. There are two general violations to the OVERHEAD PASS: the DOUBLE HIT and the LIFT. The double hit means hitting the ball with one hand first and then the other hand. Lifting the ball means catching it—even slightly—and then bringing it back up. In this case, it looks as if the setter were pushing the ball rather than hitting it. By getting your hands in the proper position, you will avoid the double hit and the lift.

Have the hands up early and in the shape of a ball, involving as many of the fingers as possible. If you need help remembering to get your hands up early, you can make a triangle with your index fingers and thumbs and sight the ball through it. If you automatically sight the ball through the triangle, you will be in the correct position each

Setting the ball

The hands should be in a ready position before the set.

time. However, it's more important to be comfortable, so if this position doesn't feel good, don't use it.

Disregard the comfort factor when it comes to positioning your thumbs; they should never be forward or they will cause the ball to shoot off in various directions. Some people prefer to have their

Some players sight the ball through a triangle to help remind them where their hands should be.

thumbs back toward their eyes, which gives them more accuracy because it allows them to hit more on the side of the ball. But if the thumbs are even with the rest of the fingers, they create a more solid set. Choose whatever feels best for you, but try to surround the ball as much as you can. Usually if a player is having trouble setting, it's because her hands are only on the back of the ball.

The set is a hitting action rather than a catching action, so the arms should go out and meet the ball. The fact that you want to hit the ball as close to your forehead as possible makes this more difficult. Even though the arms are seeking out the ball, they aren't going far before contact is made.

THE FOLLOW-THROUGH

Although there is very little arm movement before contact, your arms should extend fully after contact is made. Some setters make the mistake of yanking their hands back after touching the ball, as if they were stung. This big error really cuts down on accuracy. Your arms must follow all the way through until they are straight.

It's very important that the arms and hands move in only one direction for this motion, and they must follow the ball. To ensure that you're doing this correctly, "freeze" your arms after completing the motion. This way you can be certain that your arms are now straight and going in the direction you wanted to send the ball.

Last, don't forget to follow through with the rest of your body. Your legs are especially important for extra power. At the end of the set, your entire body should be straight.

THE VERTICAL LINE

Once you've mastered the head and arm motion, you can start focusing on leg movement. In order to execute a successful set, you must get your body underneath the ball before you hit it. You should keep your trunk, head, hips, and shoulders in a vertical line during the set, making all adjustments with your feet. Find out where the ball is heading, and get your body over there.

Many beginning players take the lazy route and lean their bodies toward the ball. This leads to disaster. You should never find yourself in the "ostrich" position of bending at the waist and trying to set. You do want your knees bent slightly, but keep the rest of your body upright. Most of the weight should be on the balls of your feet.

Always follow through with your entire body.

FOOT POSITION

Whether you are right- or left-handed, you want to position yourself with your right shoulder clos-

The jump set

est to the net. Your right foot should be in front of your left and positioned about 18 inches away, pointing forward at your target—the left front part of the net—which means your body is facing out toward your teammates and toward the court at about a 45-degree angle. If you can get in this position, then it is easy to set forward, in the middle, and behind you.

THE JUMP SET

The JUMP SET is specifically for the hitter who comes straight up the middle—the quick hitter. The jump set is a good skill for any setter to develop and basically takes the regular set one step further.

The advantage of the jump set is that it speeds up play. For instance, if your hitter hits the ball when it's about 9 feet up in the air, and you do a regular set, the ball is going to have to travel 2 or 3 feet to get to the hitter's perfect hitting height. This gives the defense more time to react to the situation. But if you set the ball when you are about 8 feet in the air, it takes only a millisecond to get to the hitter, so there isn't much time for the defense to react. In other words, the higher you are able to play the ball, the more effectively you can run the offense.

The jump set is relatively easy to master with some practice. Timing is the key. When you see the ball coming up to the setter spot, jump up to meet it. Then use the same setting motion you would have used if you had been standing on the floor.

You are, of course, limited by the height of the pass. No matter how good your jump set is, if the ball is not coming in high enough, you will have to set it from the floor. If you have mastered the jump set, you should make sure your passers know to pass it to the top of the net. Your hitter's timing is important as well. If she is not quite there, then you should not jump. Instead, wait for the ball to drop, and give her time to get in place.

Believe it or not, if you're new to setting, the jump set is a good place to start. If you can jump set, then you can set on the floor, but it doesn't always work the other way around.

THE BACK SET

The BACK SET is used when you want the hitter on the right side of the court to hit the ball. Remember that when you're in the setting position, you are facing the left front corner of the court. Rather than turning around to set the ball to the player on the right side (thereby telegraphing your intent to the entire opposing team), you use the back set.

Set up the way you would for any other set but when the ball comes at you, arch your back and thrust your hips forward. That way, when you follow through, your arms and body will all be heading in the same direction as the ball, as they're supposed to.

BALL PLACEMENT

A good set is crucial to a good offense, because it opens up all the options. Therefore, when a setter moves into position, her primary responsibility is accuracy in order to give her hitters the best opportunity to score a KILL. The sets must be accurate in all three directions—forward, backward, and the middle—to keep the attack unpredictable.

The setter should place the ball about 2 to 4 feet off the net. A common mistake among setters is that they set the ball too tight to the net, which results in the BLOCKER being so close to the ball that the hitter can't get a full swing.

How high the ball should be set depends on which hitter is getting the ball and where she is standing. The hit in the middle is called the QUICK HIT, because very little time elapses between the set and the hit due to the close proximity of the setter and the hitter. The set for the quick hit is low, about 1 foot higher than the net.

If the ball is going to the hitter in the left front corner of the court, it has to be hit with a high arc, about 8 to 10 feet in the air. A set in the same direction, but considerably closer, might be 2 to 3 feet in the air. This is the same for a back set. Experienced setters and hitters

The back set

might want to use a flat set that almost shoots across the court slightly higher than net level; however, as in the quick hit, the timing has to be perfect in order to execute the play effectively.

No matter where you hit the ball, you want to move the same way, so the defense won't know where the ball is going and won't be able to block as effectively. Good setters never give away the direction of their sets. Their position sets for backward sets is the same as for forward sets.

Know your own limitations. Never use deception at the cost of accuracy. An accurate but not tricky setter will always be more successful than a tricky but less accurate setter.

STRATEGY

As a setter, you have to be aware of where the opponent's blockers are and where your hitters are. Then you have to make the correct decision and give the right hitter the ball at the right time. Here are a few setting guidelines to help you figure out who gets what when:

1. If it's MATCH POINT and you have a weak hitter on one side and your ace hitter on the other, send the ball to your ace hitter, no matter how predictable that may seem to you.
2. If it looks as if a ball is going over the net instead of to the setter spot, save it and bring it back into the court, even if it's not going to be a great set. Any set is better than letting the ball float over to the opposing team. By saving the ball, at least you have a chance to get a hit in. If you let it go, the other team gets an easy shot.
3. If your opponent has a weak blocker, hit the ball on that side. Continue to hit it on that side until the other team can stop you.

THE OVERHEAD PASS AS A FIRST HIT

Of course, the overhead pass is not limited to the set; it also can be used on the first hit. As mentioned in the last chapter, the overhead pass was used all of the time before the forearm pass was developed. Most players have better control over the overhead pass than over the forearm pass, so it's an appealing option if the ball is coming in high.

DRILLS

1. The first drill is used to practice the fundamentals of setting. Players divide into groups of two, each with one ball. Stand about 15 feet away from your partner. If you are beginners, one person in your pair should be a tosser while the other person sets. Switch positions after 20 sets. If you are fairly good ball handlers, then you both should try to set back and forth to each other.

   While doing this drill, you should key on each of the basic points of setting one at a time. For instance, to start you can focus on going out to meet the ball. Next you can focus on hitting the ball near your forehead or making sure your follow-through is straight.
2. Juggling is a popular activity in soccer, and it should be in volleyball too. Volleyball players use overhand passes to juggle. This drill requires two players and one ball. The players begin in the setup position, approximately 15 feet apart. Player A begins by tossing the ball to player B. Player B hits an overhand pass back to player A, and the two continue passing the ball back and forth

In this drill, pass the ball back and forth as many times as you can without allowing the ball to fall below your shoulders. Always use proper technique.

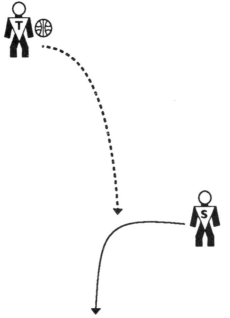

Drill 2, same setter spot

without allowing it to fall below their shoulders. If either girl is forced to dig the ball (with a forehand pass), return the ball with just one hand, or if the ball hits the ground, the drill must start over.

Repetitious training creates proper technique. Find a partner and count how many good passes you can make without missing. Try to hit 50 straight!

3. When setting, you'll have to move right, left, forward and backward to get underneath the ball so that your body can remain in a vertical line. This drill helps you practice moving to make a set, and it is similar to the second drill in the last chapter.

In that drill, you stood in the middle while your partner threw the ball to different spots. You had to return to the middle each time. In this drill, the ball always goes to the same spot, but you move. This drill simulates game play because the passers in a game always will attempt to send the ball to the same setter spot, and you won't always be there. So, in this drill, you move up, hit the ball, and then take three steps back. When the ball comes again, you move up, hit the ball, and then move three steps in another direction.

4. Once you feel comfortable setting, you can move on to other drills. This one is like the butterfly, but everyone is using the overhead pass. Basically, you follow the ball to the next position after you've hit, and two balls are going at a time.

The first player stands in the back of the court and uses the overhead pass to send the ball up to the setter spot. Then she runs up to stand in the setter line. The person in the front of the setter line sets the ball to the third spot, the hitter target, and runs to the end of that line. The target sends the ball over the net to the person at the back of the other side of the court, and she runs to that same location. The drill breaks down most often at this time, but if the players can keep the cycle going, it is a great warm-up.

This drill won't work unless you can keep at least two people in line at each position. And the players really have to be thinking. Often the two balls will catch up to one another. To avoid this, have the players slow down one ball by hitting it slow and high and speed up the other one by hitting it low and fast.

5. The next one is called the fan drill, and it is excellent for giving the setter a variety of balls to try to set. Again, there is a tosser, a setter, and a target, all on the same side of the court.

The tosser stands in the back left corner of the court to start, and she feeds the ball to the setter. The setter executes a perfect set to the target, whose position never changes. Then the tosser takes

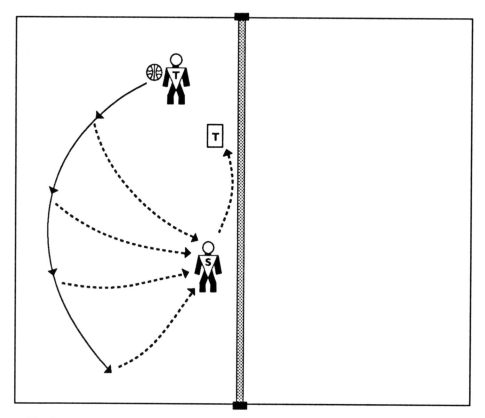

Drill 5, fan. Tosser fans around court so setter receives passes from different directions.

a step or two to the right and feeds the ball from there. The tosser eventually fans all of the way around the court so the setter gets practice having passes come at her from different directions. The line of entry changes, but the set stays the same.

6. Most players like the overhead pass game. Divide up into two teams, one on each side of the net. You must hit the ball overhead style, and it must cross the net on only one hit. The drill basically looks like a bad volleyball game in which the players have no concept of teamwork.

   The ball continues to go back and forth until someone misses. It quickly becomes obvious where the weak spot is, and then that person gets a lot of much-needed practice. The game should be played to 15, just as in a real volleyball game; when you get to 7 or 8, the front row should switch with the back row.

7. This drill is for developing the fundamental skill of back setting (passing the ball backwards). Three girls stand in a single-file line,

Back-setting is a difficult skill to master. Repetitious training is the only path that leads to consistent execution.

approximately 15 feet apart from one another. Player A holds the ball and faces players B and C. Players B and C face player A. Player A tosses the ball in the air to player B. Player B back sets the ball to Player C, who catches the ball. Player B turns around to face Player C. Repeat the drill. Have the players rotate positions until each has performed 10 backset passes.

A quick reminder: arch your back toward the target and thrust your hips forward when executing a back set.

8. It's important for setters to look the same whether they're hitting forward or backward, and this is a good drill for that. A setter and two targets, one in front and one behind, stand near the net. A fourth person tosses the ball and, while it's in the air, calls out "front set" or "back set." The idea is to force the setter to position herself the same way, no matter where the target is. She won't know which set she's doing, so she won't be able to cheat one way

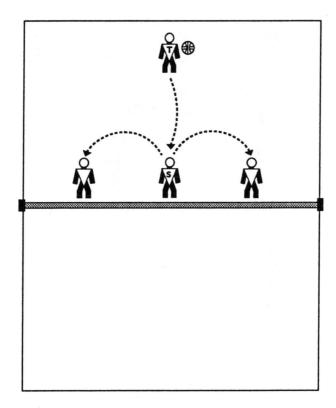

Drill 8, exercise to force setter to position herself same way, no matter where target is.

or the other. Blockers will pick up on the slightest movement, so the setter has to learn not to telegraph a set with the body. Good setters learn that they should just concentrate on getting into position before the ball gets there.

6

THE SPIKE

The volleyball floats gently through the air with the eyes of 12 people on it. The tension mounts. What will happen next? Pow! The offensive arm has whipped through the air, connecting with the ball and sending it over the net like a torpedo. In a split second, the ball has hit the floor. A point is scored, and the defensive team barely had a chance to react. The perfect SPIKE has just been executed.

The spike is the culmination of the attack. Occasionally it occurs on the second hit, but most often it is used on the third. It can be hard or soft, straight down into the court or flying through a BLOCK and out of bounds. No matter what the spike looks like, the objective is to score a KILL.

THE ARM SWING

To learn a good spike, you should begin with the arm swing. It's called a bow-and-arrow swing, because at the start you pull your arm back in the same kind of motion as when you would shoot an arrow. Your arm is bent, your elbow is back, and your hand is by your ear. Then it changes. If you were shooting a bow and arrow, your next move would be to shift your fingers and release the arrow. The rest of your body wouldn't move. That's hardly the case with the spike.

As you swing through with the spike, it changes from being a bow-and-arrow move to something closer to the whole-body movement of a baseball throw. Your shoulder is back at the start, and then as you move your arm forward to hit the ball, your shoulder comes forward, followed by your hips and the rest of your body.

(Left) The bow-and-arrow position for the spike

Don't get carried away with the baseball comparison. The arm motion and follow-through are where the similarities between a spike and a baseball throw begin and end. For one thing, you're trying to jump at the same time that you hit the spike, and baseball players do not jump when they throw. And instead of releasing a ball into the air, you are meeting a ball that's already in the air. Last, when you throw a baseball, you release the ball by your ear, but when you spike, the idea is to hit it as high above and as far out in front of you as possible while still maintaining control.

Control is the key. A spike will be difficult to dig no matter where it's

(Above and next page) Putting it all together.

sent, but a perfectly executed spike will be close to impossible to field, and that's your goal. You certainly don't want to risk sending the ball out of bounds.

MAKING CONTACT

Part of developing control over your spike is finding the perfect contact point—and there's a trick to it. If you're right-handed, look straight ahead and then straighten your left arm out and place your bicep over your left eye. Then flop your right wrist over your left hand. That's where your right hand should go every time you spike. Do the opposite if you're left-handed.

In a good spike, the first part of the hand to touch the ball is the heel. The fingers follow through, but they aren't really involved. With the serve, your wrist should be firm. With the spike, it needs to be loose. Your wrist snaps through or over the ball to provide topspin and give the ball direction.

The closer you are to the net, the more topspin you can put on the ball. Topspin is good because it will send the ball down into the court. If you're farther out, however, you have to hit the ball more in the middle; if you hit it on the top for topspin, you'll probably end up sending the ball down to the floor before it crosses the net.

An easy trick for finding the contact point

Making contact

FANCY FOOTWORK

Once you understand the arm motion, you have to learn to bring your feet to the ball. Timing is everything with the spike, so it's important to know how many steps it's going to take to get over to the ball and get up in the air with your jump.

Every hitter is different. You have to figure out the number of steps that is most comfortable for you. The one thing that is consistent, generally, is the finish. For instance, most right-handed hitters come in with a right-left finish. Therefore, a three-step approach giving you this type of finish would be left-right-left, and a four-step approach would be right-left-right-left. On that last step, bend your knees and push off for the jump.

Make sure that your last step isn't too big. If it is, you'll end up with your body going forward rather than up in the air. Your last step should be small but powerful. Plant that foot hard, and send your body in a vertical direction.

When you land, keep your knees flexed, both to cushion your landing and to prepare yourself for moving quickly into something else. Land with both feet at once, to maintain balance, and try to land with your legs spread apart at shoulder width. That gives you more mobility for a quick transition.

FACING YOUR RANGE

As you move, you want as much of the opponent's court available to you as possible. This is called FACING YOUR RANGE. If you're right-handed hitter, face the back right corner; if you're a left-handed hitter, face the back left corner.

Sometimes, facing your range will feel contrary to your natural instinct. Let's say you are a right-handed hitter on the right side of the court. If you want to hit the ball to the back left corner, instinct would tell you to turn toward that corner, rather than face the back right corner, as you're supposed to. The reason not to turn is that if you face your body away from the rest of the court, you eliminate your options. If, instead, you face the right back corner, you can bring your arm across your body to hit to the left back. You still can hit to the right back at the last minute if the other team sets up a block in your way.

It doesn't matter what side you're on. If you're a right-handed person coming from the left side of the court, you still have to face that same right back corner. In order to do this, you've got to come in from the side. If you don't, you're cutting off the entire right side of the court. Even if you do try to backhand the ball, you won't have the power you would have if you had faced the proper corner.

THREE DIRECTIONS

Now that you know how to hit and where to face, you're up against the issue of where to hit. A principle of attacking says that the hitter should give direction to the set rather than the set giving direction to the hitter. A bad set won't leave you many options, but if you have a good setter on your team, it's your job to be in position to take advantage of that meatball hanging up in the air.

If your feet are in the right place, you should be able to send the ball in any one of three directions: down the line, across the court, or through the middle (the SEAM SHOT). You should become proficient at all three types of shot.

The first hit is a LINE SHOT. The hitter attacks on either the right or left side and hits the ball straight down the sideline. The next

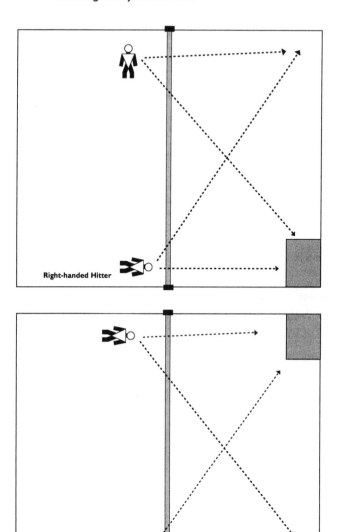

Right-handed Hitter

Left-handed Hitter

Facing your range. In order to keep as much of the court available to her as possible, the right-handed hitter faces the right back corner, and the left-handed hitter faces the left back corner.

option is the CROSSCOURT attack. This is exactly what it sounds like. The hitter receives the set on one side of the court and hits it to the opposite corner.

The last type of shot is through the middle. When blockers jump up to stop an attack, they effectively block out an area of the court. That area is called the SEAM. When blockers are not standing close enough together, they leave the seam wide open, and a hitter should take advantage of it.

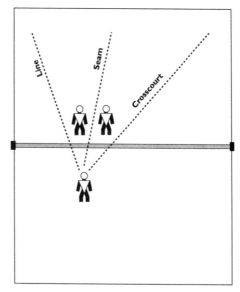

The three possible directions for a shot

An alternative to the seam is a shot called the HIGH FLAT. This is another shot right through the center of the block, but this time the hitter has no intention of getting the ball to land in the court. Instead, she is hoping that her hit will go high and hard, brushing the top of the opponents' fingers, but not being blocked by them. When the ball sails out of bounds, they will have touched it last. As a hitter, you must be sure not to put topspin on the ball for a high flat.

SOFT SHOTS

In addition to the three directions you can send the spike, you should have a number of other shots in your repertoire. One of them is called a SOFT SHOT. This is like the change-up with the serve.

Changing speeds is excellent strategy. If you give the other team only hard, fast spikes, the players will know how to defend against you. To keep the defense guessing, you want to mix some soft shots in as well. Soft shots are like drop shots in tennis, and you use them to tip the ball over the block, inside the block, or down the line. If you catch the defense off guard, these soft shots can be just as effective as the hard ones.

The percentage of hard shots to soft shots varies with the opponent. If it's a great DIGGING team, then you want to do more soft ones. The opponents are rocking back on their heels often. If you mix the hard with the soft, your opponents have to lean forward, which makes them less effective when you do come back with the hard shots. Don't worry if they are able to get the tips. In the long run you'll come out ahead because the hard shots won't be as easy for them.

Of course, if your opponents can't dig, don't even bother with the soft shots. As the saying goes, "If it ain't broke, don't fix it." As long as you're scoring points, keep hitting hard balls.

A tip shot

THE HIGH FLAT

If the blockers are in your face a lot, and you're having a tough time getting a good hit around them, try a high flat. As stated earlier, a high flat shot is a ball that has no intention of ever finding the court. Its purpose is to barely hit the top of the block and sail out of bounds. That way, opponents touch the ball before it leaves the court, and you win the rally.

Two things make a high flat shot successful. The first is proper and consistent positioning on your part, so that you always can see the blocker's hands out of the corner of your eye when you go to hit. The second is the ability to hit the high flat in any of the three directions—high line, high seam, or high crosscourt.

Also, when you're using the high flat shot, you have to be wary of the tricky blocker. If the blocker decides not to go up to block the shot, or if she drops her hands at the last minute, you have to do some last-second adjusting and hit the ball into the court, or else it would fly high and uninterrupted, right out of bounds.

Even if you aren't up against a tricky blocker, be careful not to let this happen. When you use the high flat, you have to key on hitting the block, otherwise the ball will sail out of the court with your fingerprints on it. The high flat can be tricky. You have to make sure that the ball hits enough of the blocker's hand so that the referees can see or hear that she touched it. But you don't want the ball to hit so much of her hand that she can block or slow it down.

The high flat is not used that often in high school, but the higher the level of play, the more important it becomes. If you can hit off a block as often as you hit around it, your opponent will be less aggressive and more hesitant about blocking.

THE WIPE-OFF

The last type of shot is the WIPE-OFF, and it's used when you get a bad set that is very close to the net. There are two different types of wipe-off shots, depending on where you are standing.

The first type of wipe-off is used if you are very close to the sideline. The bad set comes in, close to the net, and all you do is wipe the ball right off the blockers' hands, angling the shot so that the ball bounces out of bounds on your side of the court. The last part is key. You have to make sure the ball lands on your side; if you hit the ball off on your opponents' side and it was a simultaneous contact, they will win the rally.

The other type of wipe-off occurs when you get a bad set, close to the net, in the middle of the court. This time you want to wipe the ball off the blocker's hands softly and not at an angle. Your goal is just to bring the ball back into your court, so that you can mount another and, it's hoped, better, attack. If you're not going to get a kill, it's better for your team to have the pass-set-hit opportunity than for the other team to have it.

A final option when the set is in tight to the net is to try to push the ball between the blocker's arms and the top of the net. While this is a very difficult play for the blockers to handle, unfortunately it's also a difficult play to execute.

DRILLS

1. Too much attention is given to the act of spiking the ball and not enough care to the footwork leading up to the spike. This drill will improve your footwork on the spike approach.

   You'll need three players for this drill. The three "attackers" form a line parallel to the net on one side of the court, about 12 feet behind the net. Right-handed players should be in position with their right feet slightly ahead of their left. On the coach's signal, the attackers make a full approach and jump. Steps should be right-left-right-left, with a focus on the final two steps. The first two steps are directional steps, the final two steps should be long and explosive. Leap up and take a "dry" spike (no balls are used in this drill). A second line of three girls should immediately follow the first.

   Each player makes 10–12 approaches. This must be done at maximum effort to simulate game situations.

2. Once you've mastered the spike approach, you're ready to practice your timing so that you spike the ball at the peak of your leap with your hitting arm at full extension. To get the most from this drill it is crucial that the coach makes consistent passes—same height, same direction.

   The hitter stands approximately 12 feet back from the net. The coach stands directly in front of the net (on the same side as the hit-

Practicing your spike approach without a ball allows you to focus on footwork. Proper footwork is a prerequisite for successful kill shots.

ter), a few feet to the right of where the hitter will attack. When the coach calls out "Break," the hitter initiates her spike approach. The coach tosses the ball about 6 to 8 feet above the net. The hitter leaps up and spikes the ball over the net. She must hit five consecutive successful spikes to move on to the next drill.

The timing for each individual will vary. Girls may hit the ball when it's a half-foot above the net, one foot above or even two feet

The coach stands just to the right of the attack point. As the hitter approaches, the coach lofts the ball above the net. The hitter leaps up and spikes the ball over the net. Timing is critical.

above the net. Height, leaping ability, and arm length all factor into when and where contact is made.

3. Once you are familiar with the spiking movement, you can move on and try to hit at a target, which is the focus of this drill. Hitters should divide into two lines, each with their own set of balls, on each side of the court. A cone, a chair, or a similar item is used as target. First the hitters try for line shots. A setter in each line feeds sets to the hitters, and they have to hit the target. Once everyone in line has hit, the target is moved for crosscourt hits. Since there are two lines, this can become a competition to see which team hits the target more often.

4. It's time to practice the spike with a complete, multiple attack. This is a six-person drill, with a tosser, a setter, two hitters, and two passers. A tosser stands right next to the net on the other side (for safety's sake, because that area probably won't be hit by the spike) and throws the ball over the net to one of the passers. The passer passes it up to the setter. The setter can then set it to one of

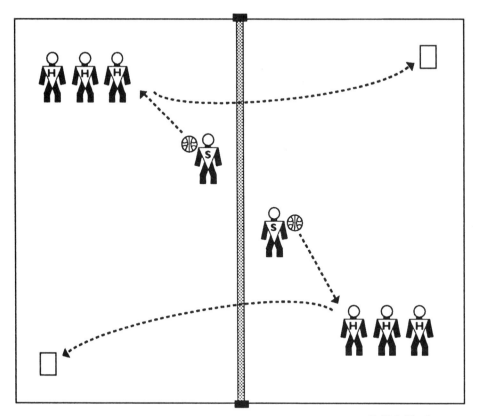

Drill 3, hit the target.

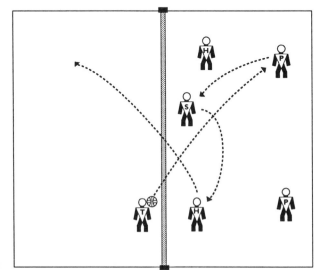

**Drill 4,
multiple attack**

the two hitters, who hits it in any one of three directions. The hitter then chases after her hit. She gives the ball to the tosser and takes the place of the passer. If the passer makes a bad pass, however, then she, not the hitter, chases down the ball and goes back into her passing position without getting a chance to hit.

5. With more people, you can do a similar drill by dividing the players into five groups—tossers, passers, setters, hitters, and shaggers. The first tosser in line throws the ball to the first passer in line, who sends it up to the first setter, who sets it to the first hitter, who spikes it over the net for the first shagger to retrieve. Go through the same pass-set-hit sequence until everyone in line has participated and then the lines rotate. Each group should have a turn in each position.

6. This two-person drill is used for developing soft shots (tips). A setter and hitter stand on the same side of the net. Two targets (cones, chairs, or X's on the floor) are placed on the other side of the net. One should be placed for a line shot or crosscourt shot and the

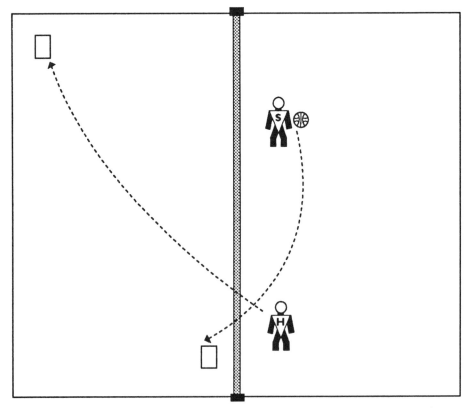

Drill 6, exercise to teach hitter to go up the same way, whether it's for a spike or a tip.

other for a tip. The setter tosses the ball, and while the hitter is in the air jumping to hit, she yells either "spike" or "tip." The hitter has to react at the last second and make the proper shot.

The point of this drill is to make all your shots look the same. You should go up planning to spike every time. If you think about tipping before you do it, most likely you'll give it away every time. You'll practically walk in, you won't jump very high, and your arm will be straight rather than in the bow and arrow. The most difficult tip to defend against is one that looks like a spike. Where you put the ball doesn't matter as much as how you deliver it.

7. The last drill involves hitting both the wipe-offs and the high flat shots. For this exercise, you have a setter, a hitter, two blockers, and a shagger. Hitters should do 10 spikes, and then everybody rotates, until each player has had a chance at each position.

The hitter shouldn't hit a high flat every time, because then the blockers will be able to key on these and stop them, and the hitter will not feel as if she has mastered the skill. Instead, she should plan to make about half of her hits high flats, mixing them up as she pleases.

7
THE BLOCK

There's nothing better than leaping into the air, just as your opponent is pounding a powerful SPIKE across the net, and then stuffing it back in her face. That satisfying move is called a BLOCK.

The beauty of the block is that it doesn't count as one of the three hits. That means you can use it as a potential weapon without much risk. Unfortunately, in girls' high school volleyball, the block isn't as much of a factor as it is in college volleyball or in boys' high school volleyball, because girls generally are not as tall. Nonetheless, blocking is an important skill to practice, and if it can be developed into a real weapon, then your team will have a huge advantage.

THE THREE FUNCTIONS

The first and most obvious use of the block is to stop the opponent's hit (stuff block). At worst, you make the other team mount another attack; if you are a superior blocker, at best you can block the ball straight down for a KILL.

The second function of the block is to slow down the ball to enable an easier transition (touch block). Since the block doesn't count as a touch, you can get your hands in there and control or slow down the hitter's attack. It's an especially good strategy to use if the opponent's hitters are better than your blockers. If you've made this determination, your blockers don't have to pay attention to stopping the ball at all. They can just focus on redirecting it.

The last reason for using the block is to reduce the area the back-row players need to cover. Defense is a coordinated effort between the back row and the front row, and blockers can manipulate the hitters toward one part of the court, by jumping in the way of another part of the court. Usually the blockers want to take away the hitter's favorite shot. Sometimes it's not clear, but often you can get some pretty good information about hitter tendencies after only a couple of hits. And, if hitters are able to go only one way, then you want to block that direction and force them to go a different way.

ON THE MOVE

Most likely you'll be moving before you jump, because unless the opposing players are really bad, they are not going to hit the ball right where you are standing. Two different ways to move to get you into position are fairly popular: the SIDESTEP SHUFFLE and the CROSSOVER. They are just like the movements used to get into position to make the FOREARM PASS.

The movements for the block differ from those for the forearm pass only because the area you have to cover is so much smaller. Otherwise,

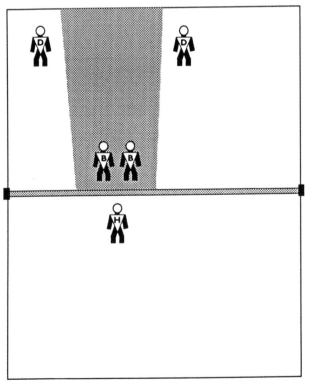

Using a block to reduce the area back-row players need to cover

Seal the net when you block.

it's the same idea. To block a near ball, one that's maybe 5 or 6 feet away, use the side-step shuffle move. Take a step, plant, and then jump.

The crossover is used for balls that are farther away. You start with the foot that is closest to the direction you are going. For instance, if you are going to the right you start with the right, cross over with the left, plant, and jump straight up.

PLANTING

Many people have trouble with the totally vertical leap. Blocking requires that you jump up high and above the top of the net; but you have to make sure you jump correctly. It's not a leap, the way a hitter might jump. You don't have to worry about which step comes first. That's because the most important part of the blocking jump is planting your feet.

When you use the sidestep shuffle or the crossover to get in position, your natural inclination will be to let your momentum continue to carry you. You can't allow this to happen. After you move over to get to your blocking position, be sure to plant your feet before you jump. If you don't, you'll jump in one place and land in another, creating a hole.

This is a real problem, because the back row will be expecting a tight block and won't be worrying about the area you're supposed to be covering. If, all of a sudden, there's a hole, you can be sure the opponent's hitter will go for it, and you could lose the rally.

The key to planting is keeping the weight on the inside of the foot on your braking step. This has an equalizing effect, shifting your weight back in the other direction, so you'll go straight up and down.

SEAL THE NET

In addition to the vertical leap, in order to be a good blocker you must be able to SEAL THE NET, meaning that your jump should be as close to the net as possible. You should be so tight to it that there's no way the ball can fit between your hands and the net. If you're square to the net—meaning that both shoulders are equidistant from it—you'll cut off a lot more area.

THE ARMS

When you jump, carry your hands high. Everything is moving so quickly that you won't have time to bring them up later. You have to keep them up all of the time, available to block, especially for situations in which the ball goes from SETTER to hitter very quickly. Even if it goes to a

Penetrate over the net if you can.

slower-tempo hitter, you might jump at the quick hitter first and then have to move over to get the girl who actually got the slower set. If you don't have your hands up already, you aren't going to be able to block.

If you're tall enough, then you can penetrate onto the other side with your arms. Unlike tennis, you are allowed to cross the vertical plane of the net, and, in fact, you should. As soon as you are able to get over the net on your jump, you should penetrate.

If your elbows can go higher than the net—a rather unusual occurrence in high school volleyball—then your arms should be more horizontal than vertical. Shrugging the shoulders will help the penetration. But don't swing your arms. Reach with them.

Hand position depends on the situation. The closer you are to the hitter, the more you can have your hands together so the ball can't go through your arms. But if you aren't right on the hitter, then you spread the hands a little to cover more area. Don't get too technical about your fingers.

SPLIT-SECOND DECISIONS

Blocking is a cat-and-mouse game. What makes it interesting is that you have to make many split-second decisions without much information. A common mistake that blockers make is keeping their eyes on the ball—but that comes later. To start, they have to watch both the setter and the hitter to see what they give away. There are a few things for blockers to key on.

For the setter:

1. Watch her hands. They might indicate which way the ball is going, although good setters will be difficult to read.
2. Look for body language cues that will tip you off. For instance, some setters will straighten their arms if they're going to do a short set for a quick hit.

For the hitter:

1. Notice what direction she is going. Eighty percent of the time—and this is fairly significant—the ball is hit in the direction that the hitter runs, so you should front the hitter. Get in her angle of approach.
2. Key on the hitter's shoulders. Even if she turns her body in the air, her shoulders will turn toward the path of the hit.
3. Last, try to keep an eye on her arms and hands as well. Some really good hitters may be facing one direction and be able to WIPE-OFF the ball in another direction altogether.

Only about 10 percent of all high school volleyball players can predict accurately, so if this strategy is getting in the way of effective blocks, just plan to block line or block crosscourt and don't bother trying to read where the hitter is going.

GETTING IN POSITION

As soon as possible, get your body over to the point of attack. If the setter isn't very good, you may be able to use the setter keys above to figure out where to go even before the set, but most of the time you'll have to wait until after the set. Usually you will begin by standing in front of the quick hitter. As soon as you see that she is not going to get the ball, you move over to block whoever will be hitting. If the quick hitter is getting it, then you jump up and try to block.

Once you're in position, you have to know when to jump. Most of the time you want to jump just after the hitter jumps, but not always. The closer the ball is to the net, the sooner you jump, because it won't take much time for the ball to cross the net. You also have to know your own jumping capabilities as well as those of the hitter. Do you have a slow or a fast jump? Does the hitter have a fast or a slow jump? These two factors will make a key difference.

If the unthinkable happens and the ball gets by you, land and turn your back to the net in the direction the ball went. At least you'll be able to see what's going on with the ball and be ready to mount an attack.

ONE-PERSON BLOCK

Often you will find yourself trying to block the shot all by yourself. This is called, for obvious reasons, a one-person block. In a one-person block, the wider you can spread yourself, the better you'll be able to block. Don't worry too much about leaving the middle open, because in general, hitters will send more balls around you rather than through you.

Another tip you might want to keep in mind is that hitters tend to hit more balls crosscourt rather than down the line. If you hedge toward the crosscourt side for the block, you might gain an advantage. (Of course, the converse of this is that if you're the hitter, watch for blockers who hedge crosscourt. They'll give you a free shot down the line.)

DOUBLE BLOCK

A double block is much harder but, obviously, it's more effective if it works. The main difficulty arises because two people have to coordi-

Double block

nate their movements. To make this easier, blockers are assigned an area. Most likely there will be a center blocker and one blocker near each end line. Depending on which hitter is getting the ball, an end blocker moves in to make the double block. If the hit seems to be directly in front of one of the side blockers, then the center blocker will be the one to move.

As a blocker, you want to move in shoulder to shoulder with the other blocker. Unlike the one-person block, there can be no gaps down the center. A good way to align yourself is to use the ball to help place your hands. You want to get the inside hand on the ball for line shots and the outside hand on the ball for crosscourt shots.

No one makes a move until after the ball has been set, so in this case the most difficult offense to defend against is the quick set. The quick hitter is already in the air before the set, so there is not much chance that the ball will be blocked. Because of that, a better strategy may be to try to touch the ball to slow it down as it goes into the back court.

STRATEGY

At the high school level, blocking is the least important skill in the game because so few players can do it effectively. At college and other more competitive levels, it becomes so crucial because the attack happens so often, and the hitters are so good, that you need a block. But no matter the level of the girls, there are a few blocking guidelines to follow:

1. Whenever you have the opportunity to get up and over early, go for the STUFF BLOCK instead of the TOUCH BLOCK. The flip side, of course, is that if you are late to your block spot, you should touch block and not worry about the stuff block. But you have to be able to read the situation to see what you have time to do.
2. Whenever the hitter does not have a good opportunity to score a kill, you should not block. Back up and let the back-row DIGGERS handle the ball. One of the worst situations in volleyball is to go up for a block and knock the ball in the wrong direction or have it hit the net because it's a weak hit. If the other team gets the ball after they've made a bad hit, you'll kick yourself.
3. If the block is helping out more than 50 percent of the time, stay with it; but if it's getting in the way, stop. For instance, if the ball is dropping between the block and the net or if the hitters are finding a hole in the block, clearly the block is hurting you.

COMMIT BLOCKING

The blocking scheme that's just been described is called READ BLOCKING. This is when the blockers wait to see where the hit is going and then move to block it. If the team you're playing, however, uses only the quick attack, the read block will be ineffective and a waste. You'll end up jumping too late and missing the hit.

Instead, you want to use a commit block scheme. In this situation the blocker always jumps with the quick hitter. "Commit" blockers don't worry about where the set is going. Their only concern is whether it's a bad pass or a good pass. If it's a bad pass, then the blocker's job is off. If it's a good pass, then the play is on. The blocker gets in the line of the hitter's approach—not even caring about the set-ter—and moves with the hitter. The blocker jumps when the hitter jumps, and she keys on where the hitter's hands go.

The disadvantage to the commit blocking scheme is that if the opponents do decide to set someone else, a double block on the side will be impossible. It's just too hard to land and get over there. There-fore, a commit block should be used only when a team's quick attack is very successful.

DRILLS

1. The first drill focuses on developing technique. In it, blockers go through the motions without the ball. Every jump should be a com-plete block, but the focus will be different. First, the blockers prac-tice sealing the net. Then they try to jump purely vertically, pene-trating if they can. Then they work on the sidestep—step and then jump—and the crossover—step, plant, and jump. Finally, they add the center blocker into the picture, so the blockers can work on their timing for the double jump.

2. The next drill involves the best kind of blocking training—re-cre-ating game situations. The first might be how to block line. A tosser can stand on a chair in the middle with two lines of hitters and two lines of blockers, one line on each side of the net, so a lot of people get to practice at once. The hitters will just hit a bunch of balls down line and the blockers will try to block them. Then the targets change, and they block crosscourt and seam. Once players have this down pat, they can practice the drill all over again with the double block.

3. If players want to work on their ability to read the set, this three-person drill is effective and fun. This drill does not have a hitter, in order to make sure players watch the setter and not the ball. A tosser throws the ball up to the setter. Then the setter varies the set, sending the ball to the right and to the left, short and long. The blocker will have to move as if she were going to block. Every time the blocker guesses correctly, she scores 1 point. Every time the setter fools the blocker, she gets 1 point. Play to 15. The winner moves into the other position, and the loser takes the place of the tosser. The tosser then fills in the leftover position.

4. This drill strengthens the technique used for blocking kill shots. Six players and a coach are needed for this drill. On one side, a

Three forwards stand in position near the net.

passer, setter, and hitter execute kill shots on offense. On the defensive side, three girls play the forward positions.

Here is how the drill works: The coach tosses the ball to the passer near the baseline who forearm passes the ball to one of her teammates. (Whoever receives the pass becomes the setter while the other becomes the hitter). The setter then overhand passes to the hitter, who leaps up for the kill shot.

As the ball is being passed, the defensive center front must anticipate on which side (left or right) the kill shot will take place. If the kill shot will be to her right, she must shift over to pair up with the right forward and help block the shot. For spikes to her left, she'll set up with the left forward. Getting set quickly is key because the two blockers must coordinate their movements. The blockers should station themselves shoulder to shoulder and keep their bodies square to the hitter. This covers the broadest and most important areas. Jump as close to the net as possible.

The offense should vary where they set up their kill shots to keep the defense guessing. After five minutes, have the offense and defense switch sides.

Once the opposing team sets up their play to the side, the center quickly moves to that side and teams with her wing player to block the shot.

5. The final blocking drill puts everything together in a gamelike situation, and it helps develop the teamwork needed for the two-person block. Basically, the setup is the same as the last drill except that you add two hitters and two more blockers.

   The tosser passes to the setter. The setter sends the ball to one of two hitters, and the blockers have to block. No quick hit is involved, so the hitters know the ball is going forward or backward. The setter shouldn't alternate, but she should mix it up so the blockers can't predict where the ball is going.

   Players have to learn to coordinate with another player and prioritize their responsibilities. They have to key on whether the setter's hands are going front or back and then move accordingly.

8
OFFENSE

Pass, set, hit! In its simplest terms, that's the offensive attack, but offensive strategy and tactics involve much more. In fact, a strategic offense is often just as important as good skills.

Before any offense is put into place, you have to understand which team is considered the offensive team, because occasionally it can get a little confusing. Sometimes the team that's on offense can't score a point, which seems contrary to what most offenses are all about. In fact, at the start of every point, the serving team is considered the defensive team, and the offensive team is actually the one receiving the ball.

What you want to keep in mind is that the offensive team is the one setting up the attack. In the beginning, the servers are considered the defensive team, because it's the receivers who are going to get the ball and then mount an attack. This team may not be the offensive team for the whole point, however. When the receiving team gets the ball over the net, then it becomes the defensive team, and the original serving team is now the offensive team.

SOME BASIC TACTICS

Offensive strategy always depends on the makeup of a team, but no matter what the team looks like, there are some tactical guidelines to follow:

1. The offensive choice should maximize the strengths and conceal the weaknesses. A team can do a variety of things on offense, and what you choose to focus on should be what you and your teammates are

good at, not what has been effective for another team or what the latest fad is. Maximizing your strengths and minimizing your weaknesses seems like an obvious concept, but sometimes it gets lost in the shuffle as teams try to use skills that they just don't have.

2. A team's competence in the SERVE RECEIVE determines what the team can do on offense. If your team can handle tough serves and pass really well, you can run an offense both next to the SETTER and away from her. But if, on the other hand, you're missing this basic skill and your team passes poorly, you can't run an attack next to the setter because the ball is usually too far off the net. In this case, you should work on developing your passing; until you have it down pat, don't try the hits next to the setter.

3. Don't employ tactically what you can't execute technically. The temptation is to try to take advantage of what the other team is giving you. For instance, if your setter has trouble setting backward, members of the other team may position themselves so that it is unusually tempting for her to set that way. But she shouldn't fall for it. Her poor sets will probably result in poor hits, and you've played right into the opponents' plan. You would have been better off sticking to what you're good at.

4. Run your offense and let the other team stop you before you make any changes. Just because opponents stop your best hitter on your first right-side attack doesn't mean you should give up immediately. Stay with something long enough to know whether it truly works or not, instead of abandoning your strength before you even get going. If, however, you do notice that something's not working, be flexible enough to try something new.

5. Get the ball to your best hitter as often as possible. This might seem too predictable, but if your best hitter is good, it won't matter how often she gets it, because she'll be able to react to changes in the defense.

6. Recognize when to go for a KILL and when not to. If you aren't going to be able to get a kill, it's better to place the ball in such a way that it's difficult for the other team to mount an effective attack. Then you might get a kill the next time around.

THE SPREAD ATTACK

The bread-and-butter attack of volleyball is the SPREAD ATTACK, in which the hitters are spread out at the net. One hitter goes out wide to the left, another goes out wide to the right, and quick hitter comes through the middle. The good thing about the spread attack is that an average passing team can use it. Everything is happening away from the setter, so if she has to move away, there are still some options open.

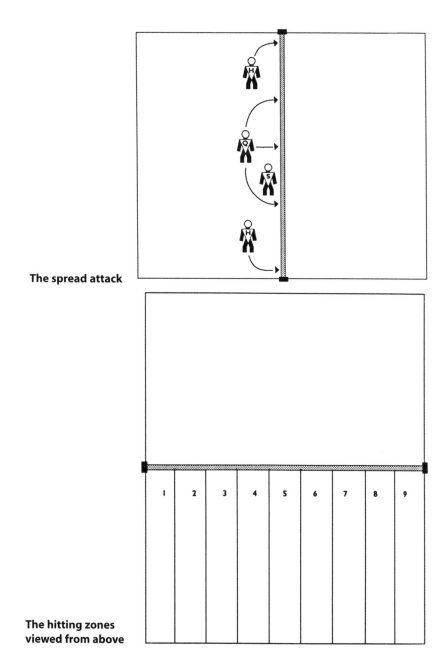

The spread attack

**The hitting zones
viewed from above**

HITTING ZONES

When a team mounts an attack, it has to choose which HITTING ZONE
to use. The term hitting zone describes where the setter is placing the

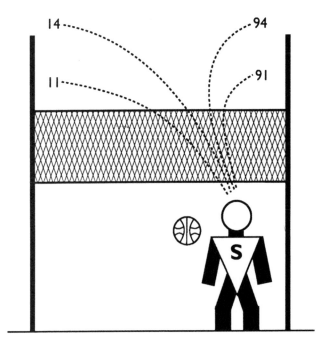

The hitting zones viewed from the floor.

ball, not the area in which the ball is going after the hit. In other words, the hitting zones are on the offensive side.

Setters use their own language and code words to communicate which zone they are sending the ball to. One such system is described here, but it's a little clumsy to use on the court. It's here because it's a very good one for explaining the basic offensive concepts.

Divide the court into the nine 1-meter zones and label each of these one through nine. The setter spot is in zone 6. To describe a hit, a two-number combination is called out. The first number in the pair is the zone the ball is going to, and the second number indicates how high the ball will be set above the net. So, for example, a 14 (fourteen) means the ball is set to zone 1 and it is 4 feet above the net. A 91 (ninety-one) means zone 9, 1 foot above the net.

Obviously some numbers will be called far more than others. The bread-and-butter options for the left-side hitter are a 14 and an 11. For the right-side hitter, they would be a 94 and a 91. For the quick hitters, they would be a 51, a 71, and a 31.

HITTING ANGLE

The left-side hitters can come in two ways for a 14: They can come in straight on a right-to-left hit, or they can come in on an angle on a left-to-right hit. The choice depends on range and what strengths the hitter has, which is a very important consideration.

If the hitter has a strong away-from-the-body swing, going with the right-to-left approach is most effective. You would use the left-to-right approach if the hitter was better at swinging across the body. For the 94 hit with the right-side hitter, it's the same strategy.

THE LOW, LONG SETS

The 11 and 91 hits are a quicker type of ball, but the set still goes out to the edge of the court. They are good hits to use if the block is bunched in the center of the court, anticipating a lot of quick hits. Your only option is to try to beat the block wide on one side or another, but you have to do it quickly. The opponents would be able to recover if you sent a 14 or a 94 out, so you want to do something faster. You want to attack before they have gotten up and over.

The set isn't the only key in this situation, however. Once you get the hit, you have to send it down the line. If you go crosscourt, you are hitting in the direction that the block is coming from, which helps out your opponents.

QUICK HITTERS

Quick hitters want to be in the air and jumping before the ball is in the setter's hands. With a 51 the hitter is coming almost right at the setter. The same is true with a 71, although the hitter is now behind the setter. On a 31, the timing is a little different. The hitter jumps when the ball is in the setter's hands. It's a very difficult set because so much depends on precise timing. Most of the time the setter, while trying to be careful, sets too slow a ball and the hitter lands before the ball gets there. A 31 takes a lot of practice.

THE X-SERIES

Another system is called the X-series. This is a slightly more difficult offense that is used to attack the gaps in the block. For instance, if the blockers were set up in the center of the court and then were beaten by some 11s and some 91s, they might spread out a little, move to the outside, and wait for those sets. This is a good time to call the X-series.

There are five different X-hits. There's a very wide one called the X1, a common one called the X2, the X3—which is hardly ever run—

The quick hit

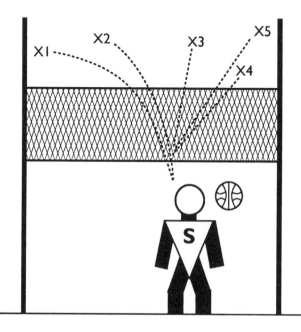

The X-series, used to attack gaps in the block

the X4, and the X5, which is pretty similar to a 94. To be most effective, the X-series is usually run in coordination with a quick hitter who is coming in for a 51.

The X1 is a set that is used when there is a big gap between the middle blocker and the right-side blocker. It's set about 3 feet off the net and is about 10 feet in from the sideline.

The X2 is a little more complicated. The quick hitter is coming in for a 51. The X-hitter wants to come in line with the quick hitter and at the last minute to break to the outside after the quick hitter jumps. The X2 is right outside the quick hitter, and if it's run properly the X2 hitter should be hitting the ball as the quick hitter is landing. It's like a piston.

The X4 keeps the blockers on their toes. It happens 3 feet behind the setter, although at first it looks like the X2. The hitter then cuts behind the setter. This freezes the block. The X5 is used later when you want to break out wider.

The X3 is a piggyback attack directly behind the quick hitter. The only time it is used is if the middle blocker was committing—jumping with the quick hitter. The idea is that the blocker jumps with the quick hitter and then is back on the floor when the X3 comes in behind her. It's a good concept, but you'll hardly ever see it run.

BACK-ROW ATTACK

Remember that the back-row players can't hit in front of the 3-meter line. They can, however, hit spikes from behind it, and they can be in the air over the line. It is also perfectly legal for them to land inside the line. Because their hits start farther out, their strategy has to be a little different.

The back row is divided into five sections: A, B, C, D, and the PIPE, which is at the intersection of B and C. The three most common hits are the A, the D, and the pipe.

For the hits behind the 3-meter line, most hitters like

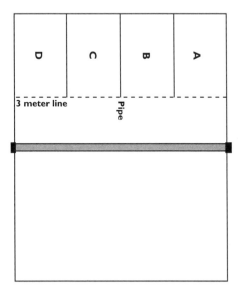

Zones for the back-row attack

The back-row attack

the ball about 8 feet off the net. This is called a DEEP SET. Of course, this means that the hitters have to be airborne before they hit it. Setting a D set is a lot like setting a 93. The same thing for an A set. It's a lot like a 14. The pipe is a lot like the X-series.

SOME STRATEGY

Once you know the basic offensive concepts of hitting zones, you can throw a little strategy into the mix. The most difficult option to stop is the quick attack, so sending two people in at the quick hit spot is very effective. The other thing that's good about the strategy is that it adds variety. If you mix up attacks, you keep the defense off balance, which adds an extra dimension to your offense. The bottom line, however, is the number of kills that an offense gets. If a simple offense move is getting kills, you don't have to be any more creative.

MISDIRECTION

If your offense does need some help, though, there are a couple of things you can do. First there's a concept called MISDIRECTION. Let's say that your best hitter is on the left, so you want to call a play to get

Misdirection. Run quick hitter to right in back of setter (misdirection), which should lead blocker away from real hit. Do opposite if best hitter is on right.

the ball there. But the opponents probably have realized that this is exactly what you want to do.

Instead, try running your quick hitter to the right, in back of the setter. This is called a misdirection, and, it is hoped, you will lead the blocker away from the real hit. You want to do the opposite, of course, if your best hitter is on the right.

BLIND-SIDE ATTACK

Another scheme is the blind-side attack. Basically, this means a hitter comes out of nowhere to take a hit. In volleyball, "nowhere" means the other side of the court. The hitter who has been hitting the 14, for instance, shifts and comes all the way around to hit a 94. It's a good scheme to use when the worst blocker of the three is over on that side.

DOUBLE QUICK SWING

The newest offense to evolve is called the double quick swing. For this play, the setter has to start in the back row, because you need three hitters in the front row for this to work.

The left-side and the right-side hitters both come in for the quick set, one at 31 and one at 51. The middle hitter then takes over their roles and is the swing hitter. She swings to the left or the right,

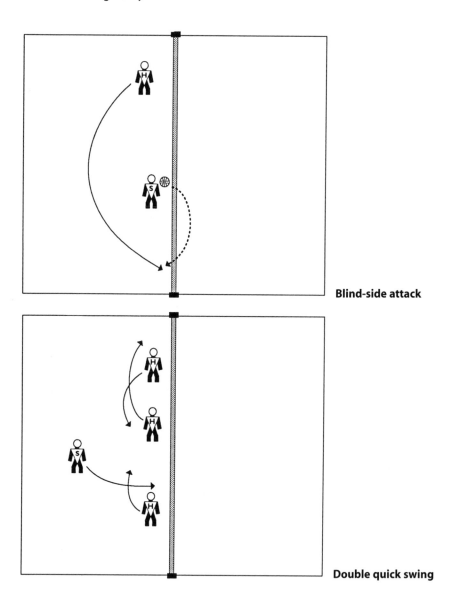

Blind-side attack

Double quick swing

depending on the situation. Some teams even use four hitters, sending the back-row hitter to the opposite side from the swing hitter.

DRILLS

1. There are a few drills to work on offense. The first is called setter-obics. Basically there are different hitting groups and a setter. Balls

are sent up to the setter, who starts off setting quick hits. After about 40 seconds she sets the left-side setters, both 11s and 14s, each for 40 seconds. Then she sets the right-side hitters, with 91s and 94s. After that, a new setter comes in. Setters can stay in for only about 2 minutes at a time before they run out of gas.

2. It's good to run a whole pass-set-hit offense when you practice. Set up with two passers, three hitters, and a setter. The hitters have their predetermined assignments, but they don't know who is getting the ball. The coach tosses the ball to the passers. Then, while the ball is in the air going from the passer to the setter, the coach should call out the type of set.

   This gives all of the hitters time to come in and jump every time. It's also a good way for the setter to practice looking the same no matter where she sets, and it's a good way to remind the team to balance the attack.

3. As soon as the offense is working nicely, make it more difficult by putting three blockers at the net. You also can add some servers and diggers to make things more interesting, but the exercise always begins again after the hit. This is to give your team a lot of SIDE-OUT work. You don't want to lose your focus by making the drill more complicated.

   If you want to make it more like a game, you can set up some sort of scoring system. For instance, make the receiving team get four side-outs before the serving team gets 2 points. This drill develops mental toughness. Getting serve after serve after serve and having to side-out on a regular basis takes its toll on a player.

4. It's important to be a versatile player because you never know when the team might need you to assume a different role. In this drill, each girl works on the three important aspects of volleyball offense: forearm passing, setting, and spiking.

   Because each player needs to concentrate solely on proper technique, no defensive players are required for this drill. The coach stands on the opposite side of the net. The passer stands near the left side of the baseline (left back), the setter is positioned near the net on the right side (right forward), and the hitter stands approximately 10 feet back from the net on the left side. The coach tosses the ball to the passer, who forearm passes the ball to the setter. The setter sends an overhand pass to the hitter, and the hitter spikes the ball for the finish.

   The players now rotate counterclockwise. The setter becomes the hitter, the hitter becomes the passer, and the passer becomes the setter. The players do not advance (or rotate) until they successfully complete the kill shot. Continue until each player produces five successful kill shots.

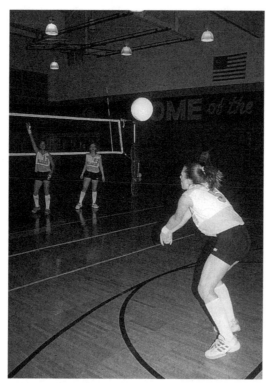

Earning a point on offense often requires perfect execution by three different players.

Each player must be a capable passer, setter, and hitter.

Any break in the chain may result in a lost point.

5. Another fun and competitive drill is called the wash. It's a two-ball drill. Ball 1 is a serve to the receiving team. The rally is played out to its conclusion. Then ball 2 is an easy toss by the coach to the serving team. If the serving team wins both balls, it scores a point. If the receiving team wins both balls, it scores a point. If each team wins 1 point, which is what happens most often, it's a wash.

9

INDIVIDUAL DEFENSE

Volleyball is a team game, and each player has to do her part or the team can't function. On defense, this is especially important. In volleyball slang, this means the players have to DIG, ROLL, DIVE, SPRAWL, COLLAPSE, and POKE. All of that translates into keeping the opponent's SPIKE from hitting the floor.

The overriding concept of individual defense is that every ball is playable until proven otherwise. The ball should never be allowed to fall. Individual defense is the one area that really shows which players have heart. Being a good individual defense player takes less actual coordination and more determination.

It's important to include defense drills in a practice often enough to keep the players physically sharp and to fuel their determination to get to every loose ball. Even if you feel your team is sharp and all the players have the right defensive mind-set, doing the drills regularly to maintain that frame of mind is still important. This defensive mind-set is a large part of getting in shape mentally. Just like any physical training program, it's easier to stay in shape than to get back in shape.

TAKING THE EDGE OFF THE SPIKE

The purpose of the individual defense is to keep the opponent's spike off the floor. Needless to say, the dig is the most crucial skill to develop for this situation. As explained in Chapter 4, digging is just the FOREARM PASS, but the ball's angle is usually more severe as it comes in.

Digging the ball

The goal of the dig is to pop the ball up high and as straight as possible, so everyone on the team will have a chance to get into position to ATTACK. Make sure the blockers have enough time to recover from BLOCKING and to get into a position to hit. Also be certain the SETTER has the opportunity to get underneath the ball for a good set.

If you feel you are in control, then you can pass to the setter spot, but you still must make sure that the pass has a high arc, because no matter how much control you have, the setters and hitters still will have to recover from either blocking or digging positions. You certainly don't want to send the ball up before the setter has time to get to the net. A lot of problems arise when diggers send the ball horizontal to the net—as they would on a SERVE RECEIVE—and no one is there because the setter hasn't had time to recover.

In order to do this vertical forearm pass, you have to make a slight modification from the normal forearm pass. Your arms are positioned with the elbows close together, just like any forearm pass, and they're held way out in front.

When you make contact with the ball, you should concentrate on bringing the thumbs up first and then the elbows. This will give you less of a swing and take the edge off the ball, which is what you want because the ball will rebound high enough without any assistance on your part. If you compare it to baseball, it's a little easier to understand. The dig is to the forearm pass what the bunt is to a home run swing.

You have to be even more careful to "bunt" the ball if you're playing with a low ceiling, especially if the ball is coming in very fast. Make sure you let the ball throw your arms against your body. That will take some of the momentum off it.

THE READY POSITION

As mentioned in Chapter 4, to get the body in a ready position for the dig, bend your knees deeply and get in a low-to-the-ground posi-

Getting in a ready position

tion with the feet spread wide. If your feet are wide apart, you can cover a larger area and reach a larger distance. It also enables you to get your body lower, which is important because it gives you more time to react. The leg closest to the sideline is out in front to force your body to turn toward the court. Your trunk should be leaning forward, more horizontal than vertical, and you should turn your toes in slightly, to help keep you centered while your weight is forward.

As in baseball, this ready position looks very much like a baserunner stealing a base. Most people are better at moving up than at moving down, so you'll be faster if you're already down. Speed is of the essence in digging, because the hits are usually very fast moving balls. Don't forget that the arms already have to be out in front; there just isn't enough time to move them out. A proper ready position can mean the difference between a dig and a KILL.

KEEP STILL

Some players use a little prehop to get themselves into position, but generally this isn't as effective as remaining still. Too often a hop puts you off balance. It's important to keep leaning your weight forward, and when you hop it's very difficult to do that. The weight ends up being one side or on the heels, and that's not good. There's so little time to react that you can't afford to spend it getting your balance.

In addition to the balance problem, the prehop often will throw off your timing. You may be caught in the process of hopping—either going up or down—when the spike comes over the net, and that fraction of a second could make all the difference.

POSITIONING YOUR BODY

On defense, any player who is not blocking—including the setter— should gear up to dig. Many people forget this because, in the serve receive, the setter is at the net waiting for the ball. In defense, though, the setter has to be back to dig or up in the air to block.

You want your body to be turned in toward the court and toward your teammates. By making the forward foot the one nearest the sideline, this will happen automatically. That way the whole court is open for the ball to rebound into.

If you're standing close to the net, you have a very small amount of time to react. All you have time to do is get in the way of the hit and have it ricochet off you in the direction of your teammates in the middle of the court. This can happen only if you are facing that way. If, instead, you are facing the net, the ball will bounce off you and go either back over the net or into it.

Back-court diggers want to position themselves the same way as the front-court diggers, although the greater distance they are from the net, the more opportunity they have to react. Their dig will be closer to a pass than a ricochet; having all their teammates and the whole court open to them is still helpful.

USING YOUR EYES

It's not enough just to be in position. You also have to be able to read where the ball is going. If you can anticipate the hit, you'll have just that much more of a jump on the ball.

The watching skills for digging are very similar to those for blocking. First watch the setter to see if she'll give clues as to who's going to get the ball. Watch the hitter to see where she's going to run, and then study her shoulders and arms for the hit.

At the high school level, you might want to try something a little different, because less experienced players have difficulty reading the hitters in time for it to make a difference. Since that's the case, diggers should set up in predetermined roles. One takes care of the hits that go crosscourt, another takes hits down the right sideline, and so on.

The dive

THE DIVE

A couple of other defensive techniques are used in conjunction with the dig when the ball is out of range. The first is called the dive. This is more popular among boys and men than girls and women. While most women aren't comfortable with the dive, they can cover quite a large range with it.

All you need to do is push off one foot and jump horizontally toward the ball as it heads toward the floor. You play the ball off the fleshy part of the arm while you are still in the air. You land on your hands and your chest, so you have to get that hit off quickly in order to free up your hands before your body hits the court. Try not to land on a corner of your body. The key to a good dive is to make sure you are already close to the floor before you go into it.

THE ROLL

Another method for getting out-of-reach spikes is called the roll. Girls and women generally use this maneuver instead of the dive. It doesn't have quite the range of the dive, but players are much less likely to hurt themselves. The roll is used when the ball is close but not close enough for you to get your body over to it and into a well-balanced ready position. Instead, you lean into the area where the ball is, thrusting your arms in its path. The ball bounces off the fleshy part of the arm while you're in motion. The momentum will take you onto the floor, where you roll over and up.

The roll

The collapse

The sprawl

THE COLLAPSE

The collapse is almost a last-ditch defensive technique for balls that are very close to the floor, the ones that don't give you enough time for a dive or a roll. A collapse is just what it sounds like. You collapse your entire body over toward the ball onto the floor. Keep the weight over the one leg that is to the side on which you are collapsing. Again, stay away from the corners of your body. You still want to hit the ball with both arms clasped together in a forearm pass fashion.

THE SPRAWL

The fourth defensive move is the sprawl. Again, it's used for a ball that is out of your reach and coming in low and fast. Basically, the sprawl is used when nothing else is going to work. Drop your body flat on the floor, reach out with one arm, and hope the ball bounces off it. You either make a fist or let it bounce off the back of your open hand.

The poke

THE POKE

Last is the poke, and it's the only move described here that isn't a dig. It is a high-ball technique. It's used most often when you're playing in the back row and a ball has ricocheted off the block and is coming over your head traveling in a line. To save it from going out of bounds because your teammate touched it last, you want to poke. You make an open fist by bending your fingers down to your palms and then try to make contact with the ball on the meaty part of your hand.

DRILLS

1. First is a two-person drill that focuses just on learning the basic skills. Each pair of players stands about 10 to 15 feet apart and should have one ball between them. No net is necessary. One player leaps up and hits a spike toward the other player. (If you and the teams you play are not highly skilled, then you should toss the ball rather than spike it. You should mimic what you'll see in a game.) The player who is digging takes five hits, keying on keeping the body low. Then she hits five spikes to her partner, who keys on the same aspect of digging.

   After the second player's five digs, they switch roles again, with the first digger keying on something else for five more hits. She might focus on digging high, getting her arms out in front of her, or facing into the court. The players switch again and continue like this until they practice and learn all aspects of the dig.

2. A similar drill is used for learning the different types of digging moves. The ball definitely should be tossed rather than hit this time, though, at least until the kill is mastered. To begin, the tosser throws the ball wide, long, or short, and the digger must use the dive to get to all five balls. Then they switch positions. They go through this same drill for the roll, the collapse, the sprawl, and the poke.

3. Once the skills are learned, set up a livelier situation: a three-person drill with a digger, a hitter, and a setter. The hitter and setter are on one side of the net, and the digger is on the other. The setter sets the ball to the hitter, who should hit 10 balls down the line for the digger to field.

   Not only will this exercise help a player learn to dig line, but she'll get an imprint of what it looks like when a hitter spikes down the line. It may help her read this type of situation in the game. After 10 spikes, players rotate positions. They should do the same drill for crosscourt hits after all three players have gone through the digging position.

4. The next drill in this learning progression will test to see if that imprint really worked. It takes a full team of diggers on both sides or, if you don't have 12 people, six players on one side and a hitter and a setter on the other.

   In this drill, the ball is set and the hitter mixes it up. She can hit line or crosscourt or even tip the ball for a change-up. She shouldn't just drop the ball over the net, however, since in this drill the diggers will be back ready to dig. In order to make sure of this, the setter can place the ball about 5 or 6 feet off the net. The farther the ball is off the net, the less court the hitter has available to her.

5. An excellent digging drill is a four-on-four game, with three players in the back row and one setter on each side. As in a regular game, the back three players must attack from behind the line. The one player up front is the blocker and setter.

   One team tosses the ball over the net to start the game. The ball is passed, set, and hit, just as in a regular game, although all of the hits are coming from the back row. That's what makes this such a great digging drill—most of the hits are going to be deep since they start from behind the line.

6. If your team is reluctant to dive, roll, collapse, and sprawl—and therefore is letting balls fall—this is a good drill for you.

   The coach stands above the net on a chair. A line of hitters stands on the other side. The coach sends a series of spikes over the net, down toward the line of players. The coach mixes up the type of ball he or she sends, hitting balls right at the digger and tossing balls slightly away from her. The digger has to determine whether to dig or chase.

   A player is not allowed to go to the end of the line until she has completed six digs successfully. If she lets a ball hit the court unnecessarily, then she gets docked three of her successful digs. This can be a very tiring drill for a sloppy player. When a player completes her six, she goes to the end of the line, and the next player is tortured the same way.

7. Defensive players can anticipate where a spike is coming from, but not where it's going. This is a drill that will help quicken reaction time and improve decision making.

   Three players position themselves in a defensive stance. Two players are positioned near the baseline and one player is approximately 12 feet back from the net. A coach stands on a chair and fires a baseball pass at one of the two baseline players. Depending on its location, the player must dig, forearm pass, or overhand pass the ball. The primary goal is to keep the ball inbounds and playable. Once players improve, they should attempt to direct the ball

This drill is for learning to control your return shots when an opponent delivers a spike. To do so effectively, you must consider the angle of the shot and adjust your body position to keep your shot on the court. Being prepared in the passer stance is key to handling high-velocity shots.

toward the front of the net where a setter would be stationed during game play.

The back player must make a quick judgment on whether the thrown ball will stay in or travel out-of-bounds. A fast-traveling shot at their shoulders will likely travel out-of-bounds, but one headed for their midsection is more difficult to gauge. Through trial and error, their decision-making skills will improve.

8. The three-player scramble is another drill in which the coach is up on a chair, feeding hits to diggers on the other side. In this case, it's three diggers. Players should divide into groups of three, and the drill is a competition to see who can get the most points.

The first group of three goes out on the court and receives 10 hits from the coach, who varies the balls. Some are spikes and some are tosses, and it's mixed up as to who they go to. Once the ball is thrown, however, someone has to dig it, someone has to set it, and someone has to hit it. Aside from its digging skill benefits, this is a great drill because it creates dig-set-hit opportunities, which make it more like live playing than some other drills.

The points received depend on what happened. If the three players successfully complete the pass-set-hit sequence, they get a point. If the ball goes out of bounds, then they get nothing. If they can't get off a hit, then they're docked a point. After 10 balls, the next group of three comes in and goes through the drill an equal number of times. The group that accumulates the highest number of points wins.

9. Another good drill is one called compensation. This involves three blockers and three defensive players on one side and a setter and three diggers on the other. All of the balls are hit to the side with the setter. The players dig, set, and hit, but now they are facing a full team of blockers and diggers on the other side. If they get a kill

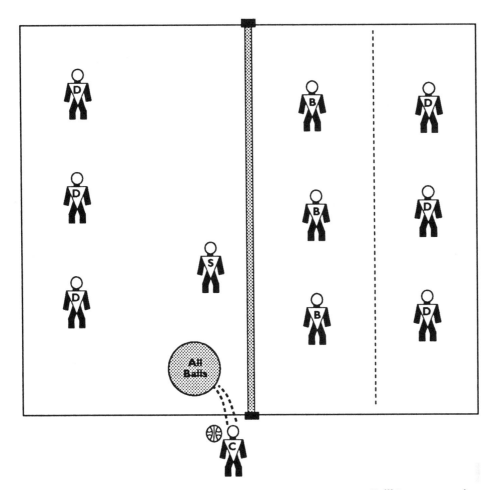

Drill 9, compensation

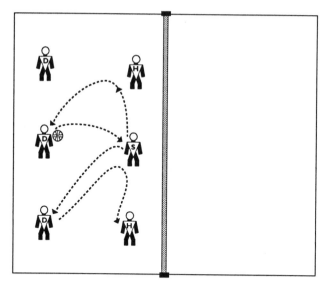

**Drill 10,
six-person pepper**

they get a point; if they go out, it's minus a point; if they get blocked or dug, it's zero.

The other team comes back if it can. However, because the setter side has no blockers at the net, the six-person team is not allowed to hit in front of the 3-meter line. If the ball goes there, it's just like going out of bounds, minus 1 point. That is the compensation. It's good to do this drill in waves of three, switching the three lines in and out and switching the setters among themselves.

10. The last drill is six-person pepper. It's a good drill for players to work on moving from their starting positions to their finishing positions, and it's all done on one side of the court.

The back row passes the ball up to the setter. The setter can either set or dump the ball slowly into the court. If the setter sets, the diggers back up. The hitter hits a medium-speed ball to the back to be dug. The ball is then dug nice and high so the setter can get to it. The setter can go back to the hitter, over to the other hitter for a hit, or just dump it back to the diggers to keep them on their toes.

10
DEFENSIVE PLAY

Unlike the offense—where you should use what your team does best and not worry about what the other team is offering—the starting defensive positions depend on what kind of team you are facing and what it's going to throw at you. Quick hitter or slow hitter? Bad SETTER or good setter? You see what type of threat the team has to offer and set up your team accordingly.

Part of setting up a defense involves coming together as a team, rather than as six independent DIGGERs and BLOCKERs. Players have to learn to work with their teammates to mount a coordinated and effective defense. This type of defensive coordination has already been touched on in Chapter 7, where the need for the center blocker and the side blockers to work together as a unit was discussed. But that's just the start. The front and back rows also have to be in sync for a defense to work.

MAKING A PLAN

Some teams wait until they see what a hitter is doing before they decide what to do defensively. This is not always a great idea even at the highest levels, but it's definitely not to be used at the high school level. The problem with waiting is that not everyone sees the same thing. It's much safer for teams to make a plan instead.

The front and back rows have a shared assignment—to cover all the areas where a hitter might send the ball. If they both try to do it all, they will surely fail. If, instead, the front row takes one area and the

back row takes another, the assignment suddenly seems a lot easier. It's always a predetermined plan, though. Before the point, the team decides, for example, that no matter what the hit, the front row is going to block line, while the back row digs CROSSCOURT.

Of course, you have to vary your plan throughout the game. Before each serve, figure out who is covering what area. While it doesn't matter who does what, having a plan is always important. That way you have a better chance of everybody executing correctly at the same time.

DEFENDING AGAINST THE QUICK HITTER

If your opponents are a good team, the attack you're most likely to see is the QUICK HIT. At the start of any defensive play against a team with

**Defending against
a quick hitter**

a quick hitter, your team should be set up as if you expect to have to defend against the quick hit. The quick attack can go sharp to the side-line or through the middle, so the players set up to stop the ball in these areas.

In the front row, the two side players should cheat in toward the center, about 10 feet in from the right side and 10 feet in from the left side. They get ready to block with the center person, who stays in the middle.

In the back row, the two players on the side move up to stand on the 3-meter line, and the middle back is all the way back on the END LINE. This is the best way to defend against the quick attack.

ONE-PERSON BLOCK

If the other team is not using the quick hitter, the one-person block defense is more appealing. The blocker blocks on one side. The back-row player on that side is behind the blocker, digging line. The other side player in the front row pulls off the net as far as she can and she digs crosscourt. The other back-row players also are digging cross-court. The front middle player moves in to get TIPs, SOFT SHOTs, and balls hit off the blocker.

Against a hitter who hits a lot of line shots, the blocker moves into the court a little more, cutting off the crosscourt, and two back-row players dig line. The opposite side front-row player and the third back

A one-person block

player dig crosscourt, basically establishing two diggers on either side of the block. The front middle layer still has the same role, looking for tips and drop shots.

Occasionally you're forced to use only one blocker when the other team has a quick hitter. This isn't the greatest of situations, but it can be done. The blocker obviously has to be the front-row middle player. The two other front people move in again, this time looking for tips.

In the back, the two outside people play deep, cutting off the angle. The middle back person is just roaming, trying to read the situation. She can go either way.

BLOCKING LINE AND DIGGING CROSSCOURT

Far more common than the one-person block is the two-person block, similar to what was used to stop the quick hit. Often it is quite successful. The idea in a defensive plan is for two people, the blockers, to shut down one area of the court, while the diggers take care of the other area.

A two-person block

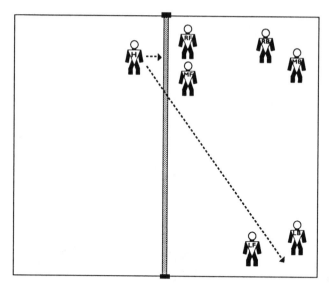

**Blocking line/
digging crosscourt**

The first situation is blocking line and digging crosscourt. The two blockers stand close to the edge of the court shoulder to shoulder. The back-row player on the same side as the block is up close looking for tips or balls that are hit off the block.

The middle back-row player positions herself in line with the inside hands of the two blockers, facing the hitter. Now she has to see what kind of block her teammates put together. If there is a hole in the block, the middle back has to move in to the middle of the court to dig, because the ball might go through the block and down for a KILL.

However, if there is no hole in the block, she wants to stand on the end line, even off the court. That way, if the hitter makes one of those high shots, hoping to hit the fingers of the blockers and send the ball out of bounds, the middle back is there to get it. Presumably, even if the blockers do manage to get their fingers on the ball and slow it down a bit, the middle back will have a chance to chase it down.

The remaining two players, one in the front row and one in the back row, are digging crosscourt. They are both on the opposite side of the court from the block. Both of these diggers are about a body length from the sideline. The crosscourt diggers' position is determined by the situation, but the front-row player pulls off no farther than 13 feet off the net.

A trick for positioning yourself for the dig is making sure that you can see both the ball and the hitter. If you can see both, that means there's a hole and the ball can get through. You're in the right position.

**Blocking crosscourt/
digging line**

BLOCKING CROSSCOURT AND DIGGING LINE

Another common scheme is to block crosscourt and dig line. The outside blocker should have her outside hand on the ball, and the middle blocker should move in shoulder to shoulder with the outside blocker. The other front person pulls off the net, looking for the short shots.

The back-row player on the same side as the block should be about 8 feet in from the end line, close to the sideline, making sure she is able to see both the ball and the hitter. This player has the toughest job in this setup. She has to be deep enough to get the line shot—that's her primary responsibility—but she also has to be aware of tips and to be able to move in if one is hit.

The middle back-row person has the same role as before. She positions herself at the seam of the block, looking for balls that are hit off the block or through the block if there's a hole. The crosscourt digger moves into the deep part of the zone to retrieve wild balls.

HITS IN THE MIDDLE

To defend against hits in the middle—X-sets and PIPES—two people dig and two people block. The middle blocker sets the block with the inside hand on the ball. The outside blocker from the side of the hit closes. The back-row player on that side moves in to look for tips. On the X-series, the rule of thumb is that if the blocker in front of you jumps, come in for tips.

The off blocker moves over toward the play and also is looking for tips if she doesn't join the block. The middle back-row player again stands at the seam of the block but is reading the play in case she has to move over to dig. The other back-row player backs up to the corner.

MOVING THE BACKS

If you're fortunate enough to have a good middle back player who's an excellent line digger, you can rotate the back row. This is good when one of your players isn't a good digger and isn't very mobile. She moves up to get the short shot and the middle back rotates over to the dig line.

The drawback is that the opposite back-row player has a little more responsibility for the deep ball, because the middle back-row player will have pulled over close to the line. You wouldn't use this scheme if the hitter goes for a lot of high seam balls, because it leaves the middle area vulnerable; but if a hitter often hits around the block, this play is good to use.

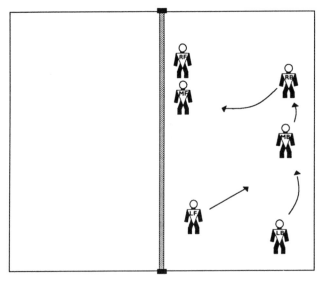

Moving the backs. If you have a player who isn't a good digger, move her up to get the short shot and move the middle back over to dig line.

Defensive setup used against a tipper

PLAYING THE TIPPER

The last two-person block situation is used against a hitter who tips frequently. Using only one player to go after the tips is just not enough, so you need to go into a two-person tip coverage.

The two blockers block line. The back-row player on the side of the block, as usual, releases up to look for tips. The second tip-retrieval player is the front person who is not involved in the block. She releases toward the block, also to look for tips.

The two people left in the back court to dig are the middle back-row player and the one in the opposite corner from the block. The middle back, as usual, stands in the seam, and the other back digs crosscourt.

THREE-PERSON BLOCK

Sometimes all three blockers are able to get into position and block the hit. When that happens, you can do one of two things. If the hitter tips often enough, the two outside back-row players can release up from the back to cover the tips. The middle back player stays behind to dig in case a ball gets through or to recover a ball hit off the block.

If the other team isn't tipping a lot, the other option is to have the two outside back-row players covering the corners and the middle player getting the tips. This is seen most often on a set up the middle.

A three-person block

No matter what the setup is, however, players using a three-person block should follow two crucial rules:

1. If you are going against a left-side hitter or a right-side hitter, do not under any circumstances let the hitter hit line.
2. Stand shoulder to shoulder, because there's not much help behind the block.

THE DOWN BLOCK

The DOWN BLOCK is not really a block at all. The play is called when it appears unlikely that the hitter will have an opportunity to score a kill with her hit. Instead of jumping up to block a hit that will be ineffective, players call a down block to free up everyone on the team for digging.

Usually the side blocker is the one to yell "down." When this happens, the front-row player on the other side immediately pulls off the net to help the dig. All three players in the back row move way back. The blocker who called the down block and the other front player pull off the net a bit to look for tips and soft drop shots.

If the setter is in the back row, she has to remember to stay back to dig instead of running up to the setter spot the moment the ball is played, which would leave a big hole in the back.

IRREGULAR SETS

Blocking line, digging crosscourt, blocking crosscourt, and digging line are defenses against good sets. However, if the other team gives its hitter a bad set, things are a little easier for you.

If your team is good at remembering different formations and reacting quickly to change, you might want to try to use the following different defensive strategies based on bad sets. But first, of course, your players have to be able to recognize which bad set they are seeing.

The Wide Set

The first is a WIDE SET, in which the ball has gone out of the court on the side. The hitter is allowed to go out-of-bounds when she hits the ball, but her opportunities for a good hit are limited by the ANTENNAE. Remember, the antennae are placed directly on the line, and the rules say that the ball has to cross on the inside of the antennae. Once the ball is outside, few options are available.

The line digger is at the best angle for seeing this bad set, and she should call "Wide." She then releases forward for tips, because it is virtually impossible for the hitter to hit line and still get the ball inside the antennae.

The blockers move out very wide, right next to the antennae, to eliminate any possibility of the hitter being able to hit the ball down the line. The blockers have to be careful not to reach over the net in this situation for two reasons. First, because they are so close to the line, the ball could easily ricochet out of bounds once it's touched; and

Setup against a wide set

second, you don't want to make it easier for the hitter by giving her the WIPE OFF option. The blockers want to be just above the net, sealing it.

The middle back person wants to shift away from the block over to the seam, and the third back wants to move up toward the net to get the crosscourt hit. The off blocker just wants to take a step off the net to dig.

The Deep Set

The DEEP SET is a ball that's set 6 feet or more off the net. This time, it's the off blocker who is in the best position to see it. She yells "Deep" and pulls off the net, looking for tips.

The rest of the team sets up in a block crosscourt, dig-line situation. If this was the team's original plan, then the off blocker obviously can completely ignore the deep set. Players already are going to be in position. But if it was opposite the original plan, then players should switch to take advantage of the bad set.

The outside blocker takes a step inside and the middle blocker moves over shoulder to shoulder. The back-row player on the side of the back gets in position to the dig line. The middle back guards against the SEAM SHOT, and the other back moves back.

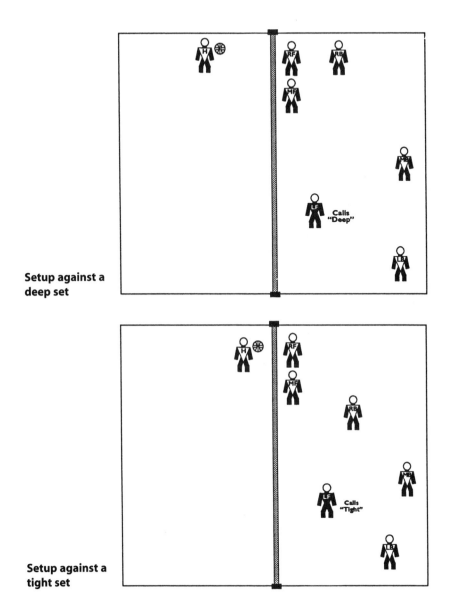

Setup against a deep set

Setup against a tight set

The Tight Set

The third irregular set is the TIGHT SET, when the set is a foot or even closer to the net. You don't want to let your opponents hit line. This will be their easiest shot because when they have to move forward that extra few feet to get the ball, their momentum is such that they still will be floating forward. Usually a forward shot is the only one available in this situation, so you want to cut that off.

Suppose that originally you were in a block crosscourt, dig-line setup, and the off blocker sees the tight set and yells "Tight." It's time to switch the plan. The outside blocker should move over close to the line, and the middle blocker should join her shoulder to shoulder. The back-row player behind the block originally was planning to dig line, but her job quickly changes. Once she can't see the hitter or ball because of the block, she moves up for tips. The others set up in a standard block line, dig crosscourt scheme.

The Inside Set

The INSIDE SET is when the hitter has intended to hit over by the line, but the set has forced her inside, closer to the middle. This now makes hitting the line shot fairly unlikely.

When the outside blocker sees this, she yells "Inside" and pulls over to the middle blocker to set the block. Under normal blocking situations, the outside blocker sets the block and the middle blocker joins it. In this case, the outside blocker joins the middle blocker, because the hitter is closer to the center of the court than near the line.

The blockers try to block crosscourt, while the rest of the team looks to dig line. The nice thing about the play, though, is that since it's unlikely that the hitter will be able to dig line, the line digger can cheat a little and move up to get tips.

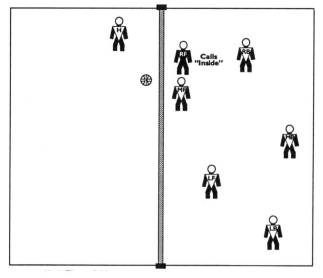

Setup against an inside set

11

TRANSITION

From about 1984 to 1988 the United States' men's volleyball team was the best team in the world. The team also happened to be phenomenal in scoring points after TRANSITION. Whenever the players came up with a ball on their side of the net during transition, they always seemed to get a strong swing into their opponent's court. In a close game, getting a couple of extra swings in transition usually means the difference between winning and losing.

Despite the apparent importance of transition, this is a relatively simple aspect of the game to explain. Transition consists merely of moving from your defensive DIGGING and BLOCKING positions to your offensive positions in an effort to mount a counterattack. Teams that can score in dig-set-hit situations rather than just pass-set-hit situations off the SERVE RECEIVE usually are the most successful.

Basically, the best way to get players used to good transition reactions is to re-create game scenarios during practice. The players start at the net and go through the different transition scenarios that they would face in a real game.

MOVING TO HIT

If you are a transition hitter, you need to make yourself available, so you must be sure to move off the net as soon as possible. By the time the ball gets into the SETTER's hands, which is going to happen quickly, you should be back behind the 3-meter line and available to mount the attack.

Moving correctly can speed up your availability. If you are a left-side blocker, you should pivot on your left foot as you land and pull off the net. It doesn't matter if you backpedal or turn and run, but you should start with that foot and end up out of bounds and past the 3-meter line. Right-side blockers land and pivot on the right foot. Again, they can back pedal or turn and run as long as they pull back beyond the 3-meter line.

If you are the middle blocker and the ball passes on the left side of the court, you should open up to the left as you pull back. Vice versa for the right side. However, if you have moved over to close a block, it's preferable to open up to the inside and pull off the net into the middle of the court.

TRAINING FOR TRANSITION PLAY

The best way to begin transition training is to start practicing the movement without a ball. The blockers work on blocking, landing, coming off the net, and then running back in to hit. The setter works on moving to the setter spot.

When players are comfortable with the proper movement, it's time to add a ball. Three blockers should stand at the net, and the setter is in the back row. They are going up against a QUICK HITTER on the other side of the net. There are no diggers. A coach or a ball tosser stands out of bounds, ready to throw in a ball.

The quick hitter jumps and simulates a hit, and the blockers try to block. Then the tosser throws in a ball. Because there are no diggers, this toss should simulate a pass and go to the setter spot. The setter should have moved up to set, and the blockers should be pulling off the net to become hitters. Go through the entire sequence—from blocking to transition to hitting—for hits from the left, the right, and in the middle.

As players master the skills, the training should become increasingly more lively. Any player can execute proper transition moves when she's not under pressure. The key to having a good transition team, though, is making sure players can do it all at top speed.

DRILLS

1. This is a one-on-one drill that is perfect for getting the basic moves down, and it's good because it not only works on the transition from defense to offense, it also concentrates on moving from offense to defense.

   A hitter and a blocker set up at the net. A tosser or coach throws the ball to the hitter to hit, and the hitting assignment is predetermined, that is, line, CROSSCOURT, SEAM. The blocker tries to block. If the hitter scores a KILL, she runs up to block, while the blocker pulls off to hit, and another ball is thrown out to the other side. If a hitter doesn't score a kill, she has to back up and get ready to hit again. The hitter scores a point only when it's a kill.

2. This next drill is a six-versus-three combination, with a coach or a tosser on the sideline adding balls. The full six-player team is on one side. On the other side is a passer, a setter, and a hitter. Depending on what you want to work on, the hitter can be a quick hitter, a left-side hitter, or a right-side hitter.

   The coach tosses the ball in, it is passed up to the setter, and the hitter hits. If the ball is dug, the six-player side plays it out. If the ball is a KILL, then the coach throws a second ball to the six-player side in the same place where the kill landed so the team can work on transition. The ball should be thrown in as soon as the kill happens, so it really feels like transition. The blockers should barely have time to land before they have to be in position.

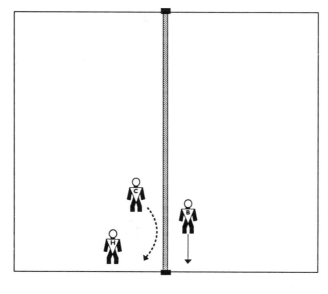

Drill 1, transition

Drill 3, quick-hitter transition

3. Quick hitters have a transition drill all their own. A passer/tosser, a setter, and a blocker/hitter should be on each side of the net. One side tosses the ball over. The receiving team sets up for a quick hit, while the blocker on the other team tries to stop it. No matter what happens, the tosser on the team that did the hit throws another ball

over right after the hit. This is the ball that the rest of the team has to be concerned with. Players take it and set up a pass-set-hit situation. The blocker has to move away from the net quickly in order to hit, and the hitter on the other team has to move in to block.

4. This drill focuses on making a quick transition from defense to offense with a predetermined strategy.

   Start with six players on each side of the net. One side is in an offensive formation and the other side is in a defensive set. The coach, standing with the offense, slaps the ball to signal a transition. The defensive team's forwards drop back to prepare to receive a free ball.

   One forward (either the right or left forward), stays at her post near the front of the net during the transition (see photo). She's the predetermined setter and becomes the target of the first pass. She sets up a teammate for a kill. It's important that the wing forward remains at her post. Otherwise, no one will be in position to set up the kill shot.

   If the team wins the point, they repeat the exercise and continue to receive a free ball. If not, the opposing team becomes the defense and is granted a free ball.

Forwards must pay close attention when the ball is on the opposite side of the court.

If they determine that the opposing team will be unable to spike the ball, they must quickly turn, run back and prepare to transition on the offense.

Two of the three forwards set up to field the volley, while the other forward stays at the net and becomes the setter.

5. This is one of the best transition drills around because it always keeps players on their toes. Two full teams set up, and a coach or a tosser stands on the side with lots of extra volleyballs.

   The first ball in play is a serve, but the other balls come from the tosser, who should sneak them in anywhere. The players don't know where the ball is going to go next, and as soon as a rally is over, they have another ball coming at them.

   This can be turned into a fun game very easily. In order to score a point, a team has to win five balls in a row. Once a team's streak is broken, the play starts over again with that team serving. The first team to reach 15 wins.

12
PUTTING A TEAM TOGETHER

More than any other sport, volleyball requires that all six players think alike and work as a team. In other sports, such as soccer, football, and basketball, the playing area as compared to the number of people on it is great. In volleyball 12 people are crammed in a very small area—more people than on the larger basketball court, for instance. With all those bodies mashed in there, players have to be able to work in unison or the game will turn into a jam worse than a six-car pileup on the New Jersey Turnpike. Getting everyone to work the same way and to see the same thing is a challenge to a coach.

The level of skill and training are important when trying to combine six people into an effective team, but usually the personalities of the players come into play too. Six very quiet people don't necessarily make the best team, even if they are the best players.

Usually it's better to have some talkers and some listeners on a team. There also should be some givers and some takers, and some aggressive people and some who are less so. Molding a compatible group of personalities takes time and skill.

THE SEVENTH PLAYER

Besides the need for a perfectly meshed group of six people, the substitutes (subs) also have to be considered. The volleyball schedule, the games, and the training are so rigorous that it's hard for six people to take the whole load. The subs are needed for the team to stay fresh and also because having extra players on the team makes for better, more gamelike practices.

When you, as a coach, are trying to place people in subbing roles, your best bet is to make sure you have a backup SETTER, a backup middle blocker, and a backup outside hitter. These are the most crucial positions. Everyone else can fill the roles of the other players. In your scrimmage training, try to mix the team makeup. Don't always put the starting six together against the subs; if you do, when you have to put a sub in a game, it's going to be tough to fit her into the team comfortably. Timing and skill level will probably drop off. Instead, you want to mix the players up. Let the subs play with the starters. Everyone should be comfortable knowing the skills of every other player on the team.

Red Auerbach, a coach of the Boston Celtics basketball team, had a subbing concept that makes a lot of sense and can also apply to volleyball. Most of the basketball teams he played against started their best five. When a sub came into the game, he usually brought down the level of play. Auerbach, on the other hand, always kept one of his best five guys off the court, and it wasn't always the same one. He thought it was more important to worry about who finished the game than who started it.

What happened is that the starters would begin the game, with one of the best five sitting out. If the team ran into trouble, the sixth player was brought in. The level of play would usually rise, and the team members might find the surge they needed to win. And if the starting five didn't run into problems, then obviously there was no need for this sixth guy.

In volleyball, it's also nice to have a seventh player who can be a pick-me-up and raise the level of play. So much of the game depends on momentum that it's good to be able to put in someone who can change the energy level of the team. This seventh player really needs to be a team player, though, one who can pull the players together when they are slipping. You don't have to follow Auerbach's philosophy to the letter, but the seventh player should add in some way, not subtract.

FINDING THE BEST PLAYERS

When looking at the possible players for your team, you have a lot to analyze—who passes well, who blocks well, who sets well, and so on. You also have to worry about things such as who is in shape and who is a leader on the court. All of these traits combine to make a good player.

Three areas of ability, when combined, seem to indicate how well a player will perform: physical ability, technical ability, and tactical ability. For instance, a smaller player who is out of shape may be able to compensate with good skills and smarts. On the flip side, a tall player may look good in the beginning, but soon into the season, you'll realize that she doesn't understand the strategy.

In the physical area, a player has to be in shape. Volleyball can be a very demanding sport, and you don't want to be stuck with a player who stops diving for balls after 10 minutes of play. Height and speed are also big pluses, but unfortunately there's not much a shorter, slower player can do to change this.

Technical ability means a player's competence in the different skills. This refers to keeping the ball under control, but it also includes having a good touch. Players have to be able to hit the ball both hard and soft, depending on what's needed.

Tactical ability is just basic smarts. A good tactical player can turn a bad situation into a good one by being aware of what her options are and how best to use them.

The degree of excellence in all three of these areas is what will determine how good a player a girl is. As a coach, you shouldn't make the common mistake of looking only at a girl's pure technical ability when deciding whether she should be part of the team.

On the other hand, almost all players will be stronger in one area than another, but under good coaching, they can work to achieve superiority in all three areas. As long as a player shows some basic competence in all three areas, her strengths of one area may be able to overcome a weakness in another. Essentially, you should look for potential.

PLAYING A ROLE

Once you pick the team, you then have to decide who plays what position. Olympic-style volleyball has six people on a team. These are the left, right, and center backs and the left, right, and center forwards. The team rotates so that everyone ends up playing each position, but that doesn't mean that everyone fulfills every role on the team. Even though the players have to be in position at the start of the play, once the ball is touched by the server, players can go anywhere.

This shifting of positions applies predominantly to the setter. Most teams have only one setter, and she wouldn't do her team much good if she were stuck in the back left corner, trying to set from there. Thus, no matter where she is, she moves to the setter spot once the play is in motion. And the middle blocker who is in the left front, for instance, will just switch with the person next to her once the ball is served. That way teams can have players specialize in their skills.

THE SETTER

The setter really is the key to the offense, so no team can ever be without one. Sometimes teams even go so far as to have two setters on the court at once, but usually it's just one.

The setter's job is to get the ball to the right hitter at the right time. Accuracy is the most important skill, so that the hitters can get good swings; as a coach, you want to look for accuracy when choosing a player to fill this position.

The second most important thing that you should look for is mobility and agility. The setter has to be able to chase down balls and bring them into controlled situations for her hitters. She also has to be able to block effectively enough and then recover to set during transition. Last, but least crucial, she should be able to DIG and SERVE. Basically, in the setter, you are looking for someone who can do everything.

Setters also need to have a certain personality. They're givers—like the point guard on a basketball team who is responsible for most of the assists instead of the points. They don't get the glory of the KILL themselves, but their reward is seeing the hitter get a good kill because of a good set.

They have to be able to make split-second decisions. They have to understand how to use the offensive concepts and then be able to use them to their best advantage. They have to be cool under fire, because their position is such a mentally demanding one. They have to be aware of who their hitters are, who is hitting well that day, where the other team's blockers are, what kind of matchups are working, and what kind of offense is working. They can't afford to lose their cool or their concentration.

THE MIDDLE BLOCKER

The next position is the middle blocker position, and there should be at least two of these on the court at a time. The best bet for a middle blocker is someone who can be as intimidating as a center in basketball. Most of the time the middle blocker is the one who hits quick sets and who blocks in the center. The best middle blockers are the ones who really enjoy blocking. Aggressiveness, jumping hard, and the ability to reach over the net every time are requirements.

Blocking is the most intimidating part of the game, so an excellent blocker really can affect the other team's offense. There's a syndrome in volleyball called avoiding the block; this is when a player is so afraid of being blocked that she hits low-percentage shots.

Essentially that has the same result as a STUFF BLOCK; even if your middle blocker isn't getting the stuffs, it will help if she's intimidating.

Physically speaking, middle blockers have to be big enough so that they can match up against the opponent's quick hitter and get over the net. They also have to be mobile enough so they can move and set blocks with the other two blockers on the outside. They have to be smart enough so they can watch the setter, anticipate what she is going to do, and then react to what she has done.

THE SWING HITTER

The third position is called the SWING HITTER, and usually two players fulfill this role. Despite the label, the most important skill for a swing hitter is the ability to pass serves. The second most important skill is the ability to swing out of the passing spot into whatever attack role the team may have. Mobility is the key when picking swing hitters. Most of the time they block on the side, which means they have to be big enough to cover two quick offensive players.

These players have to be the team's mentally toughest people, because receiving every serve is a huge burden. Players need to be tough just to be able to last a match, not to mention a season. Great passers don't prove themselves in a drill or one match, but over time. That's the real test for these positions.

THE OPPOSITE

The last position is called the OPPOSITE. This is the player who is opposite the setter. When the setter is in the back row, the opposite is in the front row, and vice versa. She should be your best hitter because, when the setter is in the front row, there are only two hitters who can hit inside the 3-meter line. The back row suddenly becomes important, and you want a really good hitter there.

The flip side works just as well, however. If, for some reason, you can't put your best hitter in the opposite position, you can put your worst hitter here, because she is always with two other hitters in the front row, so her hitting won't be needed as much.

But let's assume you are able to put your best hitter there. Opposites should be people who can hit successfully against a two-person block. They also can get the ball in the back row when the setter doesn't have a lot of options. Because of this, the opposite is often the person who scores points in TRANSITION.

THE SUBS

There are two other positions: the front-row sub and the back-row sub. The front-row sub goes into the front row for hitting and blocking. Usually this person is good at these skills but a liability in the back row. The back-row sub enters the game to serve and to give the team help with digging. Usually this player is someone with excellent digging skills. She can come in, do her job, get the team on the right track, and give it momentum.

Usually the subs come in late in the game and fill in for the weakest front- or back-row players. A sub will play all three positions across the row and then come out. Using a sub could be that extra boost your team needs at the end of the game.

The subbing rule varies according to where you are playing. In high schools and colleges a total of 12 subs are allowed, and a player can go in and out of the game three times.

Subs play less of a role in men's volleyball. For men a total of six subs are allowed, and a player can go in and out once.

MAKING THE NUMBERS FIT

When developing a lineup, a coach has to keep several things in mind. Every team needs at least one setter. For the serve receive, a team ideally should have two to five passers. Of course, it's virtually impossible to find a team that has five passers who can pass well and are of equal ability, but you never know. The minimum, however, for both men and women is two. Most high school and college women's teams consider the minimum to be three, because the net is lower in the women's game, which means there's a lot more surface area for the serve to land.

The ultimate criterion that you should use for determining how many passers you need is your evaluation of the players' skills. It's better to have two great passers take all of the court than to have two great passers share part of the court with a mediocre passer. The one who is not so good will end up getting everything, and it will hurt your team more than if you had only two passers. But if you have three good passers, go with three.

A team will need at least two middle blockers. If there are only two, one should be in the front row and the other in the back row. It's possible to have as many as six, though.

Believe it or not, hitters are down on the list. Coaches used to put their two best hitters opposite each other so that when one was in the back row, the other was in the front row. Now things have changed a bit. For instance, the 1989 Stanford University men's team had the two leading kill scorers in the country, and they stood right next to each other.

SETTING UP THE TEAM

When you're trying to assemble a team, first put in your setter and your opposite. Then take a look. Those players should give you some clues as to who else you want with them. For instance, if your opposite hits very well from the left side of the court, you want a middle blocker to her right and the swing hitter to her left. This system will allow your opposite to hit from the left twice. If the reverse is true, and your opposite is better from the right, then you switch the middle blockers and swing hitters.

Most players prefer to play the ball on one side or another—for most it seems to be the left. When you set up for a game, obviously you want to put those who are able to pass on the left on the left and those who are better passers on the right on that side.

PICKING A SYSTEM

Volleyball has created a terminology for describing the makeup of a team. Basically, it consists of two numbers. The first is the number of attackers, and the second is the number of setters.

The most commonly used system in high school is probably the 4–2. In this system, there are four hitters and two setters. The setters are opposite each other so that one is always in the front row. The advantage of this system is that it is uncomplicated and easy to execute. The disadvantage is that first you need to find two competent setters, and second you are limited to only four hitters.

Another popular system is the 5–1, five hitters and one setter. In this system, the middle blockers hit quick almost all of the time, and the opposites hit on the right and the left and out of the back row. The advantage here is the bonus of the extra hitter, and the fact that if you only have one good setter, that's all you'll need. The disadvantage is that the one setter has to take care of all the sets, and sometimes this isn't ideal.

The 6–2 is probably the most ideal situation, but not many teams are able to achieve it. In this system, there are two setters, one in the front row and one in the back row. The reason the team can count six attackers is because either setter can be part of the attack when she is not setting. In order for this system to be effective, though, both setters also have to have good hitting skills, which is why the system isn't used as often as the others. It's rather remarkable to find two players who are both good setters and good hitters.

Looked at in a different way, though, the 6–2 might turn a weak team into more of a powerhouse. If a team has two great players and the rest are only mediocre, this is a good setup to use, because those two will be handling most of the balls. It will allow the front-row setter to be the right-side blocker and the back-row setter to play defense. The back-row setter can handle the first ball and then the front-row setter can handle the second.

Another way to use the 6–2 is to have the back-row setter take all of the sets. That creates three front-row hitters, which gives your team a nice advantage.

Figure out what works best for your team. Usually the lineup you start with isn't the one you end up with. The season is just one long experiment. While you might decide early on who the best six players are, it still could take a long time to figure out who goes where.

13

GAMES PEOPLE PLAY

As is the case in most sports, to be good at volleyball you need athletic ability, practice, dedication, practice, desire, and more practice. But the nice thing about volleyball is that it's a sport people can have fun with even if they aren't world-class players. What's a picnic without volleyball?

Certainly the game as it is played internationally and in high schools and colleges can be watered down to become a very enjoyable casual sport. This chapter lists a number of related games that all evolved from the parent sport of volleyball. Even top volleyball players might have fun with these variations or use them to focus in on certain skills. They can turn a dreary practice time into a fun, competitive game.

ON THE COURT

Shuttle

In the game of shuttle, four or more players are divided into two equal teams, one team on each side of the net. The players line up one behind the other. Only a third of the court should be used, because a single person must cover the entire playing area. This is a good game to play if you have limited space and a lot of people, because you can have three games going on one court.

The first player from one line serves to the other side. Then she runs to the end of her line. The first player in line on the opponent's team returns the ball and runs to the end of her line.

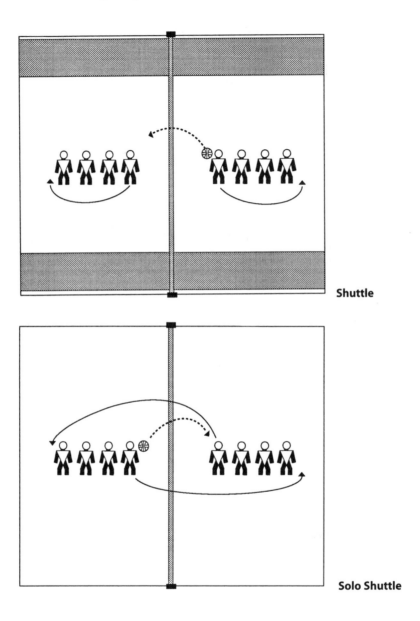

Shuttle

Solo Shuttle

The new front person is now the one who fields the serve return, and she runs to the end of the line as well. In other words, a player gets one shot and then lets her teammates handle the rest until she moves to the front of the line again.

If a player misses the ball or doesn't get it over the net, she is eliminated. The last team to have a player in the game is the winner.

This game can be changed to work on different aspects of the game, such as requiring that all hits be two-hand OVERHEAD PASSES or FORE-ARM PASSES.

Solo Shuttle

For solo shuttle, you need at least six players, but the setup is identical to shuttle, with two teams lined up on opposite sides of the net in a small, sectioned-off strip of the court. In this game it's not necessary that the teams start off exactly equal because they'll be changing all the time anyway.

Play begins, as before, with one player serving to the other side. This time, however, the player goes to the end of the line on the opposite side of the court. Every player is out for herself. There are no teams.

Again, when a player misses a shot, she is eliminated. The winner is the player who still is on the court after all the others have been eliminated. When play gets down to only two players, they don't switch sides.

Target Serve

Target serve is a serving game for two or more advanced players, and it's a great way to turn serving practice into a good game.

Players divided into two equal teams, one team on each side of the net. A target, such as a cone or a chair, is also set up on each side. It doesn't matter where the target is placed, but it should be in essentially the same spot on both sides. Basically, the placement of the target depends on whether the players' goal is to work on down the line serves, crosscourt serves, deep serves, short serves, and so on.

Teams alternate serving across the court toward the target. If the target is hit, then that team scores 1 point. If the ball hits the net or goes out of bounds, then 1 point is subtracted. No points are given or subtracted for a good serve that does not hit the target. The first team to score 15 wins.

OFF THE COURT

Crosscourt

Everybody loves crosscourt. It keeps people moving constantly, and it even can be very challenging for good players. Actually, getting the game set up in the first place can be the biggest challenge.

Crosscourt requires four nets, put together in the shape of a cross. They all share the same center pole and then radiate outward at right angles.

While crosscourt can be played with as few as eight players, the more people the better. Players divide into four equal teams and set up in each of the courts created by the four nets.

One team begins with a serve to any of the other three courts. The players on that court then hit the ball to any other court, with the rules being identical to regular volleyball. The differences arise in the scoring and the fact that each team is playing against three other teams rather than just one.

In this game, points are negative. When one team reaches 15 points, it has lost, and the game is over. The team with the fewest points at this time is the winner.

Points are given when the ball touches the ground, is hit out of bounds, or isn't sent to a new court within three hits of the ball. After a point is scored, the serve rotates clockwise to the next court.

To make this game more challenging for better players, a second or even a third ball can be added. This is not a good idea if there are only a few players, but with large groups, it makes it much more fun and fast-paced.

Wall Serve

Wall serve is the perfect game for beginning players or players who are trying to develop a new serve. At least four people are needed for this game. Players divide into two teams and stand in front of a wall. A service line is marked on the floor, and a net line 10 feet high is marked on the wall. Both teams stand behind the service line at the start of the game.

When play starts, the first player in line serves to the wall. As soon as the serve is released, the second player in each line runs forward toward the wall. The serve must be over the line on the wall, and the second person must catch the rebound. If this happens, the team gets 1 point.

Now the second player runs with the ball back behind the line to serve. The third player in line is the one who tries to catch it. As in real volleyball, the first team to reach 15 wins.

Nameball

Setting the ball is one of the most important skills a volleyball player can learn, and nameball is a good game for a beginning player who is learning to set. Another nice thing about it is that no net is needed to play, so a person can practice it at home in the driveway, for instance.

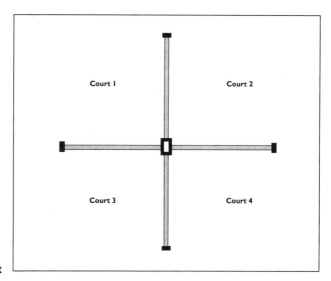

Crosscourt

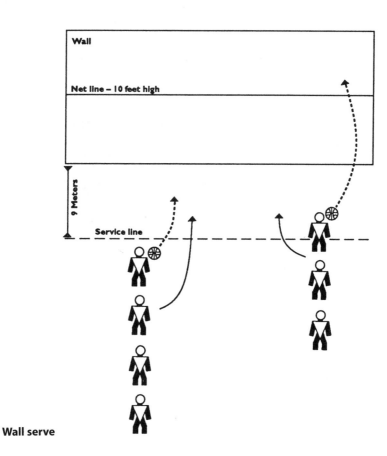

Wall serve

Three or more players stand in a fairly large circle. One player tosses the ball up into the middle of the circle and calls out the name of someone else there. That person must go into the circle and set the ball up again and call out someone else's name. The balls set up should be straight up into the center of the circle and not to a person.

This game can be played with no scoring; if players want to score, they can give points for each miss of a set. After a certain amount of time has elapsed, the player with fewest points wins.

Setter's Challenge

Setter's challenge is another setting game, but it is for more advanced players. In this game, the player sets to herself, so even one person alone can play it. It's more fun, though, when people are competing against each other.

In setter's challenge, there is a specific sequence of sets for a player to follow, and each type of set is done four times. First the player sets four two-hand overhead sets. Next she does four forearm pass sets. Then she alternates between the two for four sets. Then she sets, turns in a circle, and sets again. Fifth, she sets, touches one knee to the floor and then sets again. And finally, she sets, sits down, stands up, and sets again. All sets must be at least 10 feet high.

If a player is playing by herself, she should count how many attempts she needs before she can do the entire sequence without making a mistake. She must start over at the beginning each time.

If two or more players are challenging each other, the rules change slightly. Only one ball is used and players take turns. The first player to do the entire sequence is the winner. If a player misses one of her sets, she hands the ball to the next person and goes back to the beginning of the sequence her next time up. She does have an alternative, however. After the fourth set in a group, a player may call "I'm stopping" and hand the ball to the next player. That means that when the ball comes around to her next, she can pick up where she left off, rather than starting all over. It's a good tactic to use when a player is getting tired or feels that she is losing control. Remember, though, that a player may call this only at the end of a group of four.

Popcorn

This is another excellent game to play when there isn't a net. It works well with larger groups. Players divide into pairs or triples, depending on what works best with the number of people. Each group should have a ball, and the players should be spread a good distance away from each other.

One player sets the ball to her partner, who then sends it back again. The object of the game is to be the team that pops the ball back and forth to each other the longest, without the ball hitting the ground.

If the skill level of the players is high, this game can be done on the run, forcing the players to move to a new spot on the floor each time they receive the ball.

ON SOMEBODY ELSE'S COURT

Walleyball

Walleyball doesn't have too many rules that are different from normal volleyball. The primary difference is the location. It is played in a racquetball court or some other similar enclosed area. The net stretches from one wall to the other and all walls are in play.

In one sense, this is an easier game than volleyball, because there is no out of bounds, but in another sense, some very different skills are involved. Players have to react to the angle of the ball coming off the wall, which is harder to read than one coming straight over the net. Also, the back walls are in play, and fielding the ball after a low back-wall hit is especially difficult.

Beach Volleyball

Thousands of people have set up volleyball nets on the beach and have played their version of beach volleyball, but there is an official version of the game.

The game is played with four people, two on each side. Games are still played to 15, just as in regular volleyball, but players switch sides after a total of 5 points.

There are still three hits to a side, but the block is definitely one of the three hits. However, the blocker can play the second ball. Perhaps the biggest difference is the fact that the players are outside in soft sand. Wind and sun come into play. The wind blows the ball, and the sun gets in players' eyes. In fact, the sun actually can be part of a player's strategy. She can hit a high lob right where her opponents can't see it. Even when they do find it, they'll be slightly blinded from having stared at the sun.

Top of the Hill

If there are many beach volleyball players, top of the hill can be a great way to get them mingling and playing on different teams against different people.

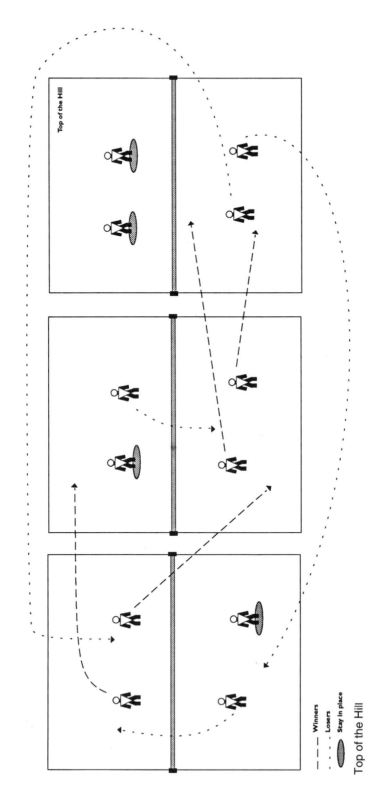

Top of the Hill

- – – – Winners
- · · · · · Losers
- ⬤ Stay in place

Top of the Hill

Square pass

The number of players determines the number of nets used. For instance, if 12 players are involved, then there will be three nets, two players on each side of the net. Each net is ranked. The highest ranked net is the "top of the hill." Players draw lots to see who starts on which court.

The games go to 5, and it's not necessary to win by 2. The winners on the top-of-the-hill court stay where they are, and they each get a point. The top-of-the-hill court is the only place where players win points. Also, players should keep track of their own points because they will not necessarily stay together as a team.

The top-of-the-hill winners stay where they are, and the top-of-the-hill losers go to the lowest-ranked net and split up, one on each side of the net. The winners of the other games move up in rank and also split up, unless they are entering the top-of-the-hill court; if so, they stay together. The losers of the other games also split up, but they remain on the same court.

Set Basketball

This game is played on a basketball court and is used to improve setting accuracy. Very simply, the object is to set the ball into the basketball net. Play starts with one person at the foul line. She sets the ball toward the basket. If it goes in, she gets 1 point. If it comes off on a rebound, another player calls for it and sets it back up. The player who calls it first gets it. If the rebound is unplayable, then another player goes to the foul line and play starts from there again. The first player to reach 15 points is the winner.

Water Volleyball

Water volleyball is the game of volleyball played in a pool. It can be played with as few as two people on each side, but it's also fun with six people on a side. The size of the pool will often be a determining factor.

Just as in regular volleyball, three hits are allowed per side, and the ball must not touch the water. If players are using a small pool with a shallow end and a deep end, they may choose not to allow the shallow-end players to stand on the floor. As this is difficult to prevent, however, it might be better to give the deep-end people an extra hit or reduce their playing area in proportion to the shallow end's playing area.

14
A FEW FINAL THOUGHTS

BEGIN AT THE BEGINNING

Now, as you're reaching the end of this book, it seems like a good time to come full circle and remind you of the overlying theme: Start with the basics and then progress. Just as you need to understand what is being said at the beginning of the book before you can understand the more advanced concepts, so do players need to be able to master the basics before they move on to the more advanced skills.

Every time a player masters a skill, she can move on to the next one; however, there's no point for a girl to try to develop a masterful JUMP SERVE, for instance, when her OVERHEAD SERVE is weak. She would do herself and her team more good if she was able to be consistent with her overhead float serve than if she could dazzle the spectators with an occasional killer jump serve.

Players with limited skills or a limited ability to read the game often complicate the play. They try difficult maneuvers when simple ones would suffice, getting in the way and often losing a good opportunity to score. Coaches and players shouldn't be confused by all the extra garbage that these players are throwing into the game. When things are not going well, you should look to the basics for repair every time. Chances are great that this is where you'll find the problem.

To put it simply, good volleyball players all seem to have two things in common. They keep their moves simple, and they all have a tremendous amount of control. Excellence in the basics often counts more than the ability to be spectacular.

SET REALISTIC GOALS

It seems obvious that when you're practicing, you need to know what your goal is, but many coaches don't even bother to find out what is realistic. Because of this, some coaches set goals that are too easy. They think they've developed good teams and then they keep losing, and they can't understand why.

Other coaches are just the opposite. They set goals for their teams that are too difficult to achieve at their level of play. This only gets them depressed and discouraged, when in reality, they are probably achieving at or above an acceptable level.

Not only that, if you don't know what realistic goals might be, you may be wasting your practice time working on a skill your team has essentially mastered. For instance, you may be spending extra time developing your BLOCKING, when your blocking success rate is higher than that of most other teams. If you researched it, statistics might show that your real weakness is the SERVE RECEIVE, which you thought was about average. Basically, you want to find out what is standard for the success levels in your playing level and practice accordingly.

Don't forget that your success rate in one area might be dependent on your skills in other areas. In the beginning, for instance, the servers are much better than the serve receivers. The serve successes will be high and the serve receives will be low. As your team gets better, the opposite will be true. Be sure to take this into account.

PLAY THE GAME

While it's tempting to use exercises and drills to develop a team's skills, good hard playing time is still the best teacher. Be sure that your team has time to play real games for a good part of practice. Only in this way will players be able to develop an understanding of how the game works.

If a player is merely doing a drill, she will not be forced to think, read the situation, and possibly improvise. Improvisation and risk taking are skills that develop only during play. Good players know when to take risks and when to play it safe, but they don't learn this from drills.

CHALLENGE YOURSELF

No matter if you're player or coach, you always should challenge yourself and your teammates to do better. Part of the appeal of volleyball is that it can be enjoyed no matter what the skill level, but the more skilled a player becomes, the more intricate, demanding, and fascinating the game of volleyball becomes.

This book has attempted to give you all the materials you need to become a competitive volleyball player or, if you're a coach, to turn your team into a volleyball powerhouse.

Follow the technique tips for each skill. Adopt the offensive and defensive strategies. Practice using the various drills. Remember, in order to play hard, you must practice hard. Above all, enjoy yourself.

GLOSSARY

Cross-references are indicated by small capital letters.

ace   Getting a point because the other team is unable to return the serve.

antennae   Markers attached to the net that rise above it to indicate the sidelines of the court.

backcourt   The area from 3 meters back of the net to the END LINE.

back set   A SET made behind the SETTER.

block (blocker, blocking)   An attempt by the defensive team to stop the opponent's attack at the net.

center line   The 4-inch line located directly under the net that divides the volleyball court in half.

change-up   Altering either the speed of the ball or the distance it travels during the serve in such a way that the opponent doesn't recognize the change immediately.

collapse   A defensive technique of hitting the ball just before it lands using a FOREARM PASS while falling to the floor.

commit blocking   A decision to block in a specific area without waiting to see if the ball will be hit in that area.

crosscourt   A diagonal direction across the court.

crossover   A method of moving quickly across the court where one leg crosses in front of the other.

deep set   A ball set 6 feet or so off the net.

dig (digger, digging)   A recovery of a spiked ball.

dink   See SOFT SHOT.

dive   An attempt to recover a ball by going to a prone position on the court.

double hit   Illegally hitting the ball first with one hand and then with the other.

down blocking   The decision not to BLOCK a shot.

end line (serve line)   The two 9-meter lines at the ends of the court.

facing your range   Setting up your approach so that you have all your options open during an attack.

forearm pass   A method of passing where the ball is hit off a platform made by putting the player's forearms together.

foul   A rules infraction resulting in a SIDE-OUT or a point for the non-fouling team.

front court   The 3-meter area back of the net.

front set   A pass that delivers the ball in a high arc in front of the setter about 2 feet from the net.

high flat   A shot that has no intention of ever hitting the court but whose goal is to fly off the fingers of the blockers and out of bounds.

hitting zones   The areas near the net where the SETTER is placing the ball for a hit.

inside set   A set that is placed near the middle of the court instead of on or near the line.

jump serve   A type of overhead serve that involves the server leaping into the air.

jump set   The player setting the ball jumps to confuse the blocker or to save a long pass that will drop over or hit the net.

kill   A hard, fast hit made at the net that is impossible for the opposing team to block or to save.

lifting   Catching the ball, even slightly, and then bringing it back up.

line shot   Hitting the ball down and parallel to the sideline.

match point   When a team is serving and is only 1 point away from winning the game.

misdirection   Sending the quick hitter behind the SETTER, thereby leading the blocker away from the actual hit.

net save   A FOREARM PASS, usually by the SETTER, made after the ball has hit the net.

opposite   The player who stands opposite the SETTER in the rotation.

overhead float serve   Method of serving in which the ball is contacted with the arm above the shoulder.

overhead pass   See SET.

pass (passer)   Sending the ball to a teammate.

pipe   A section of the court in the middle of the back row.

platform   The hitting area created by placing the arms together with elbows in close and the fleshy part of the arms facing upward.

poke   A move to save a ball from going out of bounds made by hitting the ball with the heal of the hand.

quick hit   A hit in the middle of the court using a low, quick SET.

rally   A series of plays during which the ball goes back and forth across the net several times before a SIDE-OUT or a point is scored.

read blocking   Waiting to see where the attack will come from before going up to BLOCK.

roll   A method for getting an out-of-reach SPIKE that entails leaning into the area where the ball is about to land and bouncing it off the fleshy part of the arm. After the hit, the player rolls over and comes back up to finish the follow through.

rotation (rotate)   The movement of the players after each SIDE-OUT.

seal the net   Performed by a blocker, who jumps as close to the net as possible so that the ball cannot fit between her hands and the net.

seam   The area directly between two blockers.

seam shot   Hitting the ball between the two blockers.

serve   The method of putting the ball into play at the start of each new point.

serve line   See END LINE.

serve receive   The team that is not serving.

serving box   The 3-meter designated area at the END LINE in which the server must stand.

set   A pass that places the ball in position for a player to SPIKE.

setter   The player who sets the ball to the spiker.

shuffle step   A method of moving short distances across the court where the legs do not cross.

side-out   The exchange of service that occurs when the serving team fails to score a point and the ball is given to the opponents.

soft shot (tip or **dink)**   A shot made at the net during which the ball is tipped over the BLOCK, inside the block, or down the line.

spike   A ball hit hard at the net by an offensive player.

sprawl   A defensive move made by dropping the body flat on the floor and hitting the ball, with arm outstretched, either off the fist or the back of an open hand.

spread attack   A formation in which hitters are spread out at the net with one hitter wide left, another wide right, and the quick hitter coming through the middle in one of three places.

stuff block   Blocking the ball from coming into a player's side of the court.

swing hitter   A hitter on the side of the court.

tight set   A set no more than 1 foot away from the net.

tip (tipping)   See SOFT SHOT.

touch block   Taking some of the momentum off the BLOCK so that teammates will have an easier time receiving it and mounting an attack.

transition   Changing from offense to defense or vice versa.

underhand serve   Method of serving in which the ball is contacted with the hand below the shoulder.

wide set   A set to the outside of the court near the side.

wipe-off   Hitting the ball off the blocker's hands on purpose.

VOLLEYBALL RESOURCES

http://www.usavolleyball.org, is the official website of the sport's governing body, USA Volleyball. USA Volleyball is recognized by the Federation International de Volleyball (FIVB) and the United States Olympic Committee (USOC) as the sport's governing body in the United States.

Contact information:
USA Volleyball
715 South Circle Drive
Colorado Springs, CO 80910
Phone: (719) 228-6800
Toll Free: (888) 786-5539
Fax: (719) 228-6899
Email: postmaster@usav.org

Volleyball World Wide offers information on all aspects of the sport of volleyball—from beginner to professional, grade school to college to the Olympics at www.volleyball.org. You can find a wide array of information, from the history of the game and its complete rules to how to build a sand volleyball court. It even has discussion groups about volleyball and a long list of frequently asked questions.

The FIVB (Federation Internationale de Volleyball) governs and manages all forms of volleyball and beach volleyball worldwide, through planning, organizing, marketing, and promotional activities aimed at developing volleyball as a major world sport.

Contact information:
Av. de la Gare 12
1000 Lausanne 1
Switzerland

Phone: +41 21 345 35 35
Fax: +41 21 345 35 45
Email: info@mail.fivb.ch
Website: http://www.fivb.org

http://www.uspv.com is the official web site of the United States Professional Volleyball League. Headquartered in the suburbs of Chicago, USPV will be the first women's professional indoor volleyball league in the United States.

Contact information:
The United States Professional Volleyball League
1051 East Main Street Suite 212
East Dundee, IL 60118
Phone: (847) 551-1350
Toll Free: (877) THEUSPV
Fax: (847) 551-3510
Email: contact@uspv.net

The Association of Volleyball Professionals (AVP) is an organization that promotes the interests of the world's best beach volleyball players.

Contact information:
Association of Volleyball Professionals Corporate Offices
330 Washington Boulevard Suite 600
Marina Del Rey, CA 90292
Phone: (914) 767-0600
Fax: (914) 767-0700

FURTHER READING

Bertucci, Bob, and Peterson, James. *Volleyball Drill Book: Game Action Drills.* Indianapolis, IN: Masters Press, 1992.

Bulman, George. *Play the Game: Volleyball (Play the Game Series).* New York: Wardlock, UK (Sterling), 1990.

Davis, Kathy. *Advanced Volleyball for Everyone.* Winston-Salem, NC: Hunter Textbooks Inc., 1991.

Dunphy, Marv, and Wilde, Rod. *Volleyball Today.* Anaheim, CA: West Publications, 1991.

Ferguson, Bonnie J., and Viera, Barbara L. *Teaching Volleyball: Steps to Success.* Champaign, IL: Human Kinetics, 1990.

Gutman, Bill. *Volleyball (Go for It Series).* North Bellmore, NY: Marshall Cavendish Corp., 1990.

Haley and Stokes. *Volleyball for Everyone,* 2nd ed. Winston-Salem, NC: Hunter Textbooks Inc., 1992.

Herbert, Michael R. *Insights & Strategies for Winning Volleyball.* Champaign, IL: Human Kinetics, 1991.

Loggins, Victor, and Pederson, Joe. *Bump, Set, Spike: Everybody's Volleyball Book.* Chicago, IL: Contemporary Books, 1986.

Lucas, Jeff. *Pass, Set, Crush: Volleyball Illustrated,* 3rd rev. ed. Wenatchee, WA: Euclid NW Publications, 1993.

Neville, William J., and United States Volleyball Association Staff. *Coaching Volleyball Successfully.* Champaign, IL: Human Kinetics, 1989.

Nicholls, Keith. *Volleyball: The Skills of the Game.* North Pomfret, VT: Crowood UK (Trafalgar), 1989.

INDEX